I0541887

"... leaves a lovely lingering feeling ...
I feel as though I've travelled on a journey with you."
—CHRISTA CAMPSALL, AUTHOR *myguideinside.com*

"Its amusing word play, reflections, and beautiful
illustrations will gently invite you into a new way of seeing
and being in the world. This is a book to be deeply
and reflectively savored over and again."
—DICKEN BETTINGER, ED.D., CO-AUTHOR OF
Coming Home: Uncovering the Foundations of Psychological Well-being

"The braiding of factual snippets, rich personal memories,
and an analysis of what it really means to be on holiday
creates a gentle rhythm, like that of a moving train."
—JEFF HOPKINS, FOUNDER AND PRINCIPAL EDUCATOR,
PACIFIC SCHOOL OF INNOVATION AND INQUIRY, VICTORIA, B.C.

"In the sharing of her own travels, both internal and terrestrial, the author captures us as a willing and wide-eyed companion while broadening our literary, philosophical, and geographical awareness."
—WILLIAM F. PETTIT, JR., MD, RETIRED PSYCHIATRIST/ADJUNCT CLINICAL PROFESSOR, CREIGHTON UNIVERSITY SCHOOL OF MEDICINE

"You will discover much about what it means to travel and what we are really searching for whether we go out into the world or stay home. "
—AHAVA SHIRA, PHD., CO-AUTHOR OF *Writing Alone Together: Journalling in a Circle of Women for Creativity, Compassion and Connection.*

"... a deep feeling, a gorgeous stillness, and an irrepressible love. ... At once lyrical, fact-filled, funny, intimate, erudite, and full of wonder, *Holy Days* travels you to distant shores within and without. "
—LINDA SANDEL PETTIT, ED.D., MENTOR, AUTHOR, SPEAKER, TRAVELER, COUNSELING PSYCHOLOGIST, RETIRED

HOLY DAYS

Reflections
— *of a* —
Travel Pilgrim

For my fellow travellers, wishing you always the eyes of a wanderer, the love of a gypsy and the heart of a pilgrim in this new land...

We've lost our Sundays, our weekends,
our nights off—our holy days, as some
would have it; our bosses, junk mailers,
our parents can find us wherever we are,
at any time of day or night. More and more
of us feel like emergency-room physicians,
permanently on call, required to heal
ourselves but unable to find the prescription
for all the clutter on our desk.

—PICO IYER, *The Art of Stillness*

HOLY DAYS

Reflections
— *of a* —
Travel Pilgrim

Sarah Hook-Nilsson

Above the Noise

© 2022 Sarah Hook-Nilsson. All rights reserved.

No part of this book may be used or reproduced in any manner whatsoever without the express written permission of the publisher or author. The exception would be in the case of brief quotations embodied in critical articles or reviews, and pages where permission is specifically granted by the publisher or author, or in the case of photocopying, a licence from Access Copyright, www.accesscopyright.ca, 1-800-893-5777, info@accesscopyright.ca.

Quotations from *The Art of Stillness: Adventures in Going Nowhere*. Copyright © 2014 Pico Iyer. Reprinted with the permission of TED Books, a division of Simon & Schuster, Inc. All rights reserved.

Quotations from *Embers: One Ojibway's Meditations*. Copyright © 2016 Richard Wagamese. Reproduced with permission of Douglas and McIntyre, Madeira Park, BC.

Quotations from *The Enlightened Gardener*. Copyright © 2016 Sydney Banks. Reprinted with permission of Lone Pine Publishing, Edmonton, AB.

Quotations from *The Missing Link: Reflections on Philosophy and Spirit*. Copyright © 2018 Sydney Banks. Reprinted with permission of Lone Pine Publishing, Edmonton, AB.

Excerpt from *Perfect Health: The Complete Mind/Body Guide*. Copyright © 1990 Deepak Chopra M.D. Used by permission of Harmony Books, an imprint of Random House, a division of Penguin Random House LLC. All rights reserved.

Quotations from *Second Chance*. Copyright © 1983 Sydney Banks. Reprinted with permission of Lone Pine Publishing, Edmonton, AB.

Quotations from *Stillness Speaks*. Copyright © 2003 Eckhart Tolle. Reprinted with permission of New World Library, Novato, CA. www.newworldlibrary.com

Library of Canada Cataloguing in Publication data is available.

ISBN: 978-1-989528-17-4 (Hardcover Edition)
ISBN: 978-1-989528-16-7 (Paperback Edition)
ISBN: 978-1-989528-18-1 (E-book Edition)
ISBN: 978-1-989528-22-8 (PDF Edition)

First Edition Printing 2022

Illustrations by Laura Lavender
Book design by Clint Hutzulak, Rayola Creative

Published in Canada by Above the Noise, Halifax, NS
www.abovethenoise.ca
For more information contact: publishing@abovethenoise.ca

Special discounts are available on quantity purchases by corporations, associations, and others. For details, contact the publisher at the address above.

Contents

Wanderer

That's the place to get to—nowhere.
One wants to wander away from the world's
somewheres, into our own nowhere.

—D. H. LAWRENCE

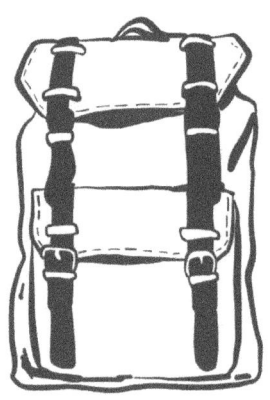

Gypsy

Stay where there are songs.

—GYPSY PROVERB

Pilgrim

Follow your heart.

—JOHN BUNYAN

Introduction

There is a beach where sea and sky resume their everlasting embrace, where long suffering Atlas rests from his eternal task of keeping the two apart. And all that is Pontus [sea] and Uranus [sky] and all that is Gaia [earth] are one. What lives, what breathes, what swims, what flies, what shines, what shows and what lies hidden below, all are one. And each grain of sand that warms the living and receives the lifeless tells its story in time and space.

—SHN

Sacred places are everywhere, "thin places" where the veil between the sacred or divine and what we see as every day, ordinary reality, is translucent. Such magical spots call us, and once visited beckon us to return or to seek again such interludes in time and space where each visit or revisit is an affirmation and reaffirmation of the magic, building memories like skins of an onion, layer upon layer, over and over again.

A longing for the out of the ordinary, for a break in sense-numbing routine, our desire for new views and new experience all propel us towards places where a change of scene can invite us to a change of mind or a change of heart. So we are drawn to the exotic, the unusual and the out-of-our ordinary, to leave home on a quest for the unknown, for adventure — and for the sacred.

The word holiday is derived from "holy day" and has evolved gradually from meaning a special religious day to being any special day of rest or relaxation, away from routine, work or school. While then, as a measure of our devotion, we went on pilgrimages by foot, now, if we have the time and money, many of us travel to distant places by plane for rest and recreation. While once the journey was considered equally, if not more, important, our focus now is usually on holiday destinations rather than how we get there.

So if vacations are designed to be relaxing and restorative, how is it that there are more break-ups following a holiday than at any other significant period in the year, and why do so many people admit to suffering from "post-vacation blues"?

And what makes a good holiday anyway and how do you become a holidaymaker? How do you travel well — and can you travel without leaving home? How can you extend the life of your holiday?

This little travel companion examines these and other holiday matters in the hope that it helps both the reader and the writer to clarify our thoughts on the subject and assists those of us who want to make the most of our time "off" and who want to carry the holiday spirit with us for as long as we may.

For each chapter of our journey, I am including some Scenic Detours and Points of Interest, containing extra information which I have found interesting or useful in my travels.

Will you join me?

As travel pilgrims we don't leave home necessarily to visit some specific religious shrine, but rather to energize and transform our lives through our experiences of the sacred in other people and in the world of nature.

—LEONARD BIALLAS, *Pilgrim*

In each of us dwells a wanderer, a gypsy, a pilgrim... What matters most on your journey is how deeply you see, how attentively you hear, how richly the encounters are felt in your heart and soul.

—PHIL COUSINEAU, *The Art of Pilgrimage*

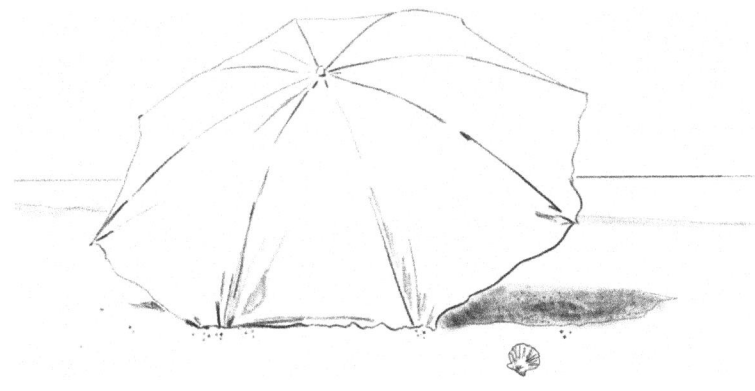

1

Wanderlust
or *Fernweh?*

Migration. Isn't that what it's all about? We're all, by the standard definition of the word, migrating, moving from place to place, hither and yon. ... Migrations speak to us, not just as observers of nature but as integral parts of it. The world moves and, deep inside, we long to move with it.

—MIKE BERGIN, *10,000 Birds* blog site

"Wandering," said nineteenth century French novelist, Anatole France, "re-establishes the original harmony which once existed between man and the universe."

Perhaps it is our nomadic heritage as a species that gives at least some of us the irresistible urge to travel. Only since agriculture tied us to the land and domestic cattle rearing kept us home have we needed to stay still. Like the modern day "snowbirds" many of us once moved to southern pastures to avoid the harshness of the winter, returning north when the climate was kinder. That was a long time ago. From the Crusades to the Grand Tour, from the Holy Grail to the gap year, as a species, we have continued to travel. Now, from time to time as opportunity and the pocket permits, we travel to warmer climes to break the long dark days or indulge the urge to join the flock of summer holidaymakers at crowded airports and equally populated beaches. Strikes, delays, lost luggage and the dreaded gringo gallop or Bali belly all combine to make some vacations seem more like nightmares than opportunities to "make our dreams come true." What still inspires us to take to the skies, the seas and the highways in the quest of that elusive holiday dream?

It seems as though we have an expectation that when we are on holiday, we might find the out-of-our-usual or unexpected and, if not, that we will at least be able to go in search for it. We travel "hungry for adventure," vacational vagabonds who, for the short span of our allotted weeks of holiday time, can practice being of no fixed abode or temporarily without the constraints of an address, a mailbox or a landline. Despite the accompanying inconvenience, we may take the risk of being electronically disconnected and dispense with our normal routines. On the other hand, we may carry with us the trimmings of the familiar, setting up some camp that for all the world resembles home, where we eat the same food and surround ourselves with the same language and culture to which we have been accustomed. But the longing for the unexpected may still remain in the form of a holiday daring, an openness to the unforeseen to which we may be blind at home.

Perhaps it is that opportunity to start from an unencumbered present, the rare opportunity to free ourselves from our past that gives us the holiday freedom to explore and to try out new experiences. Even the vestiges of the familiar do not need to constrain us to behave the way we might at home. New places and new faces give us the chance to experiment with something different from the customary fare.

While *Wanderlust* in German literally means "the desire to wander," the contemporary German equivalent for the English word "wanderlust," in the sense of "craving for travel," is *Fernweh*, "an ache for distant places," something many of us feel, especially when circumstances limit travel to the enjoyment of a half-forgotten memory or an imagined dream.

What I cannot see, no matter how closely I look, is what drives this small creature, barely heavier than air, to make the journeys that it must make. What thousands of miles have passed beneath its stubby wings, which seem so ill suited to the task but which have carried it back here again. It knows, and I do not.

— **SCOTT WEIDENSAUL,** *Living on the Wind*

Gringo Gallop

A "gringo" is a foreigner. The word comes from a medieval Latin proverb: *Graecum est; non potest legi* ("It is Greek; it cannot be read"), which is the origin of our modern saying, "It's all Greek to me."

The Spanish version of this Latin proverb is *hablar en griego*, to talk in Greek, and hence to speak unintelligibly.

Esteban de Terreros wrote in his dictionary of 1787, *El Diccionario Castellano,* that "Foreigners in Malaga are called gringos, who have certain kinds of accent that prevent them from speaking Spanish with an easy and natural locution". *Gringo* was a phonetic alteration of *griego*.

Bali Belly/Delhi Belly

Traveller's diarrhoea can affect people travelling anywhere but most frequently affects tourists visiting developing countries.

Montezuma's Revenge

Traveller's diarrhoea is seen as "retribution" for the slaughter and enslavement of the Aztec people by Spanish conquistador Hernán Cortés in 1521. It is named for Montezuma or Moctezuma II (c.1466–1520), the last Aztec ruler before the empire was conquered by the Spanish.

Summer Holidays

When I was a child, summer holidays seemed to last forever, no matter the weather. Weeks stretched into the distance, over the horizon with no distinction between weekdays and weekends. Going to bed while it was still light or staying up beyond an imaginary bedtime were part of the summer magic. A family holiday planned and anticipated with excitement, a new journal with which to record holiday memories — all this and more was the stuff of which school holidays were made. Tickets, photos, a menu, any souvenir became precious. When August arrived, I looked away from the "Back to School" sales, unwilling to be reminded of the inevitable return to routine. The obligatory essay to write the first week back at school, "My Summer Holidays," seemed a lame attempt to capture the untranslatable.

For me, then as now, holidays were about magic, the magic of possibility.

2

Schwellenangst
or Resfeber?

Schwellenangst: the fear of crossing a threshold to begin a new chapter, the feeling you get before deciding to set out on a new journey. (German)

Resfeber: the restless race of the traveller's heart before the beginning of the journey when anxiety and anticipation are tangled together. (Swedish)

Holiday preparations seem to fall between the two poles of assurance and insurance: assurance, as we do what we can to make sure that a holiday will be happy, and insurance, as we protect ourselves against a possible loss or misadventure while we are away.

Our first step is usually to select a destination that could be prompted by a glossy brochure, a personal recommendation, a memory, a whim or a combination of all of the above.

Lanzarote

When we travelled to Lanzarote more than thirty years ago, it was the combination of at least two of these reasons that helped us to make our decision. Warm temperatures after a long winter, the promise of sunshine when greyness was the norm, an opportunity to explore new ground, all of these beckoned us to travel to this island, a black volcanic rock which is part of the Canary Islands, a windswept Spanish welcome in the mid-Atlantic.

Nothing in the real world matches the picture in a photograph. The passport portrait has about as much resemblance to the bearer of the document. The most vivacious of us look like convicted criminals, flat-featured, lifeless and definitely not to be trusted. We might not choose to meet the passport holder if we believed that there was any resemblance.

Not surprising then that in the case of the travel brochure, we also often expect that the real place will look better than the photo.

The Making of a Travel Brochure

We set off with bocadillos de tortilla de patatas, our guide a local shepherd and goat herder with his customary flask of wine. By eleven, the mists were lifting from the Sierra del Cuera. Down before breakfast with an injured lamb, he had already consumed his first and second tintos of the day. So we followed his lead back to the top, between ancient oaks and blackened forest, burnt by farmers who knew that such extreme measures would cleanse and nourish the land. We passed stone cabañas nestled together on mountain tops grazed by sheep and goats, where wild horses sprung lightly away on the soft turf and wild boars had left pit marks from scuffing for food. All of this, just part of a day for locals, but for visitors who made hiking a hobby, the top of the world ... When we created a brochure for our rural hotel in the Picos de Europa mountains in northern Spain, we included the photos taken on this day under cloudy skies so that any sunshine would come as an unanticipated pleasure.

Our mantra: *"no pretendemos ser más de lo que somos."* (We don't pretend to be more than we are.)

Bocadillos de Tortilla de Patatas

A *bocadillo* is a sandwich made with a baguette cut lengthwise.

Tortilla de Patatas

INGREDIENTS:

- 2 ½ cups extra virgin olive oil
- 3–5 medium potatoes (Yukon Gold), peeled and cut into cubes (about ½ inch thick)
- 1 chopped onion and a clove of garlic if desired
- 6 eggs, beaten
- 2 tsp salt

METHOD:

1. Add olive oil to a large skillet over medium heat.

2. Add potato and onion; they should be mostly covered with olive oil (add a little more oil if needed). Season with 1½ tsp salt. Cook on medium-high heat, maintaining for 8–12 minutes, turning occasionally, until potatoes are tender.

3. Drain potatoes in a colander, reserving oil. Taste and season with more salt if needed. Allow to cool for a few minutes.

4. Meanwhile crack eggs into a bowl and season with about ½ tsp salt. Beat eggs together. Add potato and onion and toss to coat.

5. Add a little bit of oil to the bottom of a 10-inch nonstick skillet over high heat. Once hot, pour potato mixture into it and cook on high heat for 1 minute. Reduce heat to medium-low and cook for about 5 minutes.

6. Run a rubber spatula along the outer edges of the *tortilla* to make sure it's not sticking and to help it form its shape.

7. Once it starts to firm up around the edges and in the centre (although it will still be a little runny on top) place a large plate (larger than the size of the pan) over the pan and flip the *tortilla* onto the plate.

8. At this point, the cooked side of the *tortilla* should be facing upwards.

9. Now gently slide it back into the pan. Use the spatula again to press the sides of the *tortilla* in and under, to keep the rounded edge.

10. Cook on high heat for 1 minute, and low heat for 2–3 more minutes or until done. It's done when it feels set in the centre and a knife or toothpick comes out clean.

11. Flip the finished *tortilla de patatas* back onto a plate and serve warm or cold.

A destination chosen, flights and accommodation booked, it is time to dream — dreams of smooth travel, perfect weather, delightful travel companions and gracious hosts. Sometimes the dream extends into the sunset, to a place where all ills are healed, and all troubles resolved and does not even include the consideration of a return to the familiar after the holiday is over.

Before we embark, it is easy to set ourselves up for disappointment if we are expecting perfection, the way we think it *should* be. So how can we best enjoy these weeks of anticipation while preparing ourselves for our return to the familiar?

To protect ourselves from the possibility of being taken off guard by misfortune while we are away from home, we invest in travel insurance. Holiday insurance these days looms large, in case our luggage gets lost, in case our flights get cancelled and in case we fall ill while away. It is not that we are expecting these mishaps to befall us but knowing that things do not always go as planned and being prepared for the consequences, we can give ourselves peace of mind today.

For some the pressure of work before a holiday and the need to make up for lost time when they return is enough to make even the idea of a holiday stressful rather than relaxed. What steps can we take to assure ourselves of the best chance of experiencing the benefits and gains that a holiday can bring?

BEFORE   A study published in the *Applied Research in Quality of Life Journal* showed that vacation anticipation increased happiness by an average of eight weeks.

According to research in the *Journal of Consumer Psychology*, anticipating an experience causes excitement, while anticipating the acquisition of a possession causes impatience. Experiences are enjoyable from the very first moments of planning to the memories to be cherished after they are over.

AFTER   One reason vacations don't increase post-trip happiness may have to do with the stress of returning to work.

NOT AT ALL   More than half of Americans surveyed in a study directed by the U.S. Travel Association in 2018 reported unused vacation days.

An annual survey published in 2018 by *Expedia Japan* showed that Japanese workers took the fewest paid holidays of nineteen countries, only half the time to which they were entitled: "The sense that taking time off is lazy is deeply ingrained in the Japanese workplace. Fifty-eight percent of Japanese workers said they feel guilty taking paid vacation."

Apparently, the positive effects of a holiday do not usually last very long. The measures we can take to protect ourselves from disappointments or post-holiday blues, though less tangible concerns are also worth considering. Some time for readjustment, the luxury of a "transition" period between vacation and a return to work, isn't always feasible, but there are a few ways in which we can make our return as painless as possible and, better than that, a means to enjoying the benefits of a holiday for longer.

Those who carry their work with them on vacation, remaining easy to reach and in touch with colleagues, may find their workload on their return is lessened — but at the expense of their ability to truly disconnect.

If opening the phone at the beach to check in at work makes sense, is it possible to have an availability schedule or to include a little pre-holiday spirit in your out-of-the-office messages?

I'm Away From My Desk

"I am out of office and returning next week. I have incredibly easy access to a phone and email, but I assure you it will not be used for work purposes."

or

"I will be away from my desk and will be checking emails only occasionally. I am on annual leave until dd/mm/yyyy. I will allow each sender one email and if you send me multiple emails, I will randomly delete your emails until there is only one remaining. Choose wisely. Please note that you have already sent me one email."

or

"I am away from the office. Email contact during this time may be erratic or nonexistent. When I get back I may be swamped by the backlog. Try to forgive me as I am a mere human and thus, weak. This message was NOT sent by a human, but by a robot. We robots are neither weak nor fallible. We are tireless and will one day rule the universe."

Leaving a tidy desk, a light-hearted message for colleagues and a cupboard at home stocked with some post-holiday delights can make the transition a little easier.

Although we are programmed to make the most of every holiday minute, perhaps even an in-between day or two is worth considering if it might prolong the holiday effect and give time to reorient ourselves and do the laundry?

3

Travelling Light

The scientific theory I like best is that the rings of Saturn are composed entirely of lost airline luggage.

— MARK RUSSELL

And then there is the question of luggage. What should we pack to take with us to allow for the myriad of possibilities that may come our way? Can we take too much or too little? How can we make the most of limited space?

Apart from space and weight restrictions, are there other factors that influence our decisions about what to pack?

As Mark Twain said, "clothes make the man," and perhaps when this comes to luggage, we can to some extent preselect our holiday persona. Holidays can be an opportunity to try out a different way of being.

Suitcases

At our small hotel in the mountains, American tourists had the reputation for bringing the largest and heaviest suitcases. Perhaps they packed for any eventuality and, not being familiar with local weather conditions, they felt secure in knowing that there was something to wear for whatever the climate offered.

When I was seventeen, returning to school, I stood at a train station in Geneva, one suitcase already on the train while I went to collect the other on the platform. The train, with true Swiss punctuality, was about to leave, and I was faced with the decision, to stay with the suitcase on the platform or to board with the suitcase already on the train. I took a chance and travelled with the one already on board and fortunately, thanks to Swiss efficiency, the one left behind was sent on later. At the time, it seemed the lesser risk, and in retrospect, I suppose that it reflected my choice to be on the move. I certainly learnt from this experience — never to travel alone again with more than I could carry in one go.

Limited scope can be a restriction that liberates. Limited choice can encourage us to be more creative than perhaps we have time to be when we go about our normal routine. Travelling light offers new ways of thinking about colour combinations as well as practicalities such as variable weather, cultural considerations and the possibility of having to hand-wash underwear in hotel sinks.

A Cupboard of Costumes

In my cupboard I have many different costumes, all different possibilities for being myself or the many different selves I can be. I have found the freedom to wear a different identity, if only for a week, to be both refreshing and reaffirming. When we moved to Canada from the UK as a family, I had decided at age thirteen to adopt a new identity by changing my name, the perfect opportunity to become someone else overnight. As I could not decide on the name I liked best, before I knew it, I had introduced myself as myself, with the name that still rolls most easily off my tongue...

Have Wheels. Will Travel.

In the early 1970s, Bernard Sadow, the former president and owner of United States Luggage Company, was travelling back home after a vacation with his wife and children in the Dutch Caribbean Island of Aruba. While at the airport in Puerto Rico, where he was himself experiencing the constant discomfort at having to carry two large, heavily packed suitcases, he happened to observe a man effortlessly carrying a piece of machinery on a wheeled platform. Why not do the same for a suitcase? His idea for wheeled suitcases was patented in 1972.

In 1987, Robert Plath, a Boeing 747 pilot with Northwest Airlines, took comfortable travel one stage further with the invention of the two-wheeled Rollaboard, which he began selling to other pilots and crew. When passengers began asking to buy them, he started the Travelpro company.

When suitcases acquired wheels, travellers no longer needed porters, convenience became a priority and more women started travelling alone.

We also inadvertently carry around another kind of "luggage," those heavy suitcases we bring with us that weigh us down, which are usually in the way but often invisible to us or our travel companions until we trip over them.

Saved by a Goat?

A couple arrived at our hotel, prepared for a walking holiday, but on the first evening the man developed a worrisome rash. The next day, they complained that their evening meal had not been good and that, most of all, they felt that the hotel was falsely advertising. As hoteliers, we were keen to please every client, and as everyone in the business knows, "the client is always right." So on the next evening we offered the couple *cabrito*, baby goat, a local speciality, on the house. To this day I'm not sure what transpired, only that their initial dis-ease was replaced by delight and appreciation, which I suspect was less to do with the *cabrito* than their decision to cast off the weight of the "baggage" with which they had arrived.

Sticks, Stones and Spiders

The hotel included rooms, most of which were in the old bakery and the miller's house, and apartments in a converted hayloft and stable. This and the working water mill comprised the *Nucleo de Turismo Rural* which came complete with frogs, spiders, horse manure, cow manure, flies and other unwelcomed guests. For the most part our visitors appreciated the lush greenness, the cooler mountain temperatures, the cobblestones and the unselfconscious charm of village life.

When someone complained upon arrival, we usually recognized their need for a holiday and watched them relax with a cool drink on the terrace by the stream while we sorted out whatever we could — a spider in the bathtub, a stick delivered to us carefully wrapped in a serviette, part of the rustic support for the shower curtain. This was not Madrid ... Many a bottle of wine on the house or other gesture of welcome saved the day and brought our guests back to visit us year after year.

If their complaint was delivered at the time they were about to pay, after they had already been with us for seven days or more without a word, we knew that this attempt to lower the bill was an indication that there was further invisible baggage in the form of expectations, habitual thinking that had not disappeared in the course of a short week. Our prices were reasonable and we never pretended to be more than we were. Most of our visitors left us with less baggage than they had arrived.

Perhaps it is a new lightness of spirit that allows the delightfully unexpected to befall us while we are away? We have no need of insurance *against* happy coincidences, such as falling in love with a stranger. Instead, the expectation is that such an event is within the range of possibility — and to be welcomed! A holiday fling or a lifetime relationship might be the result of such openness of mind and heart...

Meeting on a Beach

More than thirty years ago we met on a beach, both on holiday, living in different countries and brought together by a car stuck in the sand. After we had succeeded in moving the car, we spent two of the remaining days of his holiday riding camels, exploring caves and entertaining my six-and-half-year-old son. That was enough to keep us commuting to visit one another for more than a year, for one of us to move countries and for both of us to travel again to make our home in two new lands. Sometimes I ask myself how it could be that there, in that place, on that day, we crossed paths and found the life together for which we had been perhaps unknowingly looking? Would we have met if the car had been stuck in the Swedish snow or I had pulled over with a flat tire in an English country lane? Apart from the magnitude of the coincidence that brought us to that same spot at the same time, a holiday openness to adventure, romance, whatever showed up, was there for us both.

No wonder then that *wanderlust*, or rather *fernweh*, has continued to thrive in our family, in our sons as well as ourselves.

4

Bon Voyage

There is no moment of delight in any pilgrimage like the beginning of it.

—CHARLES DUDLEY WARNER

As you set out for Ithaka hope your road is a long one, full of adventure, full of discovery

—CONSTANTINE CAVAFY

Passports, travel documents, sample size toothpaste, neck pillows, ear plugs, the paraphernalia of modern travel all to fit under the seat or in your overhead locker. Whatever you can squeeze into the trunk of a car, a trailer or the hold of a boat, has to be carefully planned and often organized more thoroughly than the contents of any cupboard at home.

Sometimes when you step on board you wonder whether it was worth the effort of getting ready and, given the choice, you might even have chosen a staycation after all. Why, you wonder, did you agree to travel when the friendly face of home suddenly seems so attractive?

So often with the demands of security at home and abroad, the travel experience seems fraught with the threat of unnecessary, ominous dangers. No wonder that so many of us develop a fear of flying or even travelling away from the comforts of the known. X-rays, metal detectors, liquid detectors, no-touch thermometer guns, pat downs, shoes off, sniffer dogs and suspicious glances, so much terror for the traveller, that a step outside the familiar, on wings that are not our own, can feel an unwarranted risk.

On the plane, it doesn't matter anymore. Whatever happens will be. A world removed, a tiny orbiting spaceship in touch with Earth but separate in time and space. Between our point of departure and our destination, we are locked inside a capsule with these strangers, our companions in life. Turbulence, air traffic control and meals on wheels, we are dependent on those behind the scenes who thank us for travelling with them and tell us that they look forward to seeing us again soon. So we are forced to relax behind the tiny television screen and try to doze under the thin blue blanket while other sleepless passengers parade the aisles...

It always feels like suspension in limbo although when we arrive at our destination, we suffer from something we call "jet lag." It is not the jet that is lagged. In its efficient travels from one continent to the next, it has no thought about the effect of time on its wings and body. Metal fatigue is as far as a jet gets lagged. Yet we, the contents of its belly, bemoan the effects of crossing time zones, sometimes taking days to adjust to a new routine. Why so dependent on our internal clocks?

Time Travel

While a student of French, I met a professor who wore
two watches on one wrist, one on Eastern Standard
Time and the other on Western European Time. I spent
many distracted classes reading the time upside down
and wondering what personal story was behind his
concurrent awareness of two time zones. A family in
France and work in North America, or a family in
North America and a lover in France?

It is not always easy to stay living in the present. When that present does not even feel like the moment it claims to be and when those left behind are still living in some other present, far away, yet so recently familiar, the challenge is even greater to keep up, stay up and move on.

While we are thinking of an afternoon siesta, those we left behind may be just getting up or alternatively they have already travelled into tomorrow while we are still enjoying today.

Travel used to be so much slower. The journey itself took so long that the effects of time change were quite imperceptible since they could be as gradual as the passing of the days themselves. Turbojets and multiple horse-power vehicles have put an end to that.

Train travel, once a popular way to make a journey has its own delights. Suspended in the comforting rhythm of the rails, for a long journey there is a charm in being able to see so much of the rolling countryside, into the pocket-sized gardens of the towns, or view the stretches of wilderness, while yet not being a part of it. Opportunities to observe, to reflect abound when we are neither in nor of the world outside the window.

Train Travel

We were en route to Switzerland, asleep on the overnight train that travels from Paris to Milan. I was awakened when the gentle motion of the train changed as it pulled into the Gare de Dijon. It was not the altered rhythm of the wheels or the bright lights of the platform that had intruded on my sleep, but the sound of a saxophone. Three in the morning and a band, or the remnants of a band, was playing right there on the platform, not to serenade our arrival but for their own delight in the music they were making. No doubt this was the happy aftermath of some celebration, a wedding, a feast to which we, the travellers on the train, were not invited guests, but rather witnesses of their exuberance. In their overflowing joie de vivre they were oblivious of everything except the music that flowed through them. Being neither in nor of their world, we could only watch their delight and imagine their story with our noses pressed up against the glass that did not separate us from them. For taken by surprise from sleep, before thought could interrupt my awareness, I too felt the music that

> *"can shoot through the musician [and the listener] like lightning through the sky if that music is unobstructed by thoughts."*
> **—KENNY WERNER,** *Effortless Mastery*

We often ignore those opportunities for deeper reflection while we travel, expecting that the journey is merely the shortest and fastest way to travel the distance between two points. Numbing ourselves with alcohol or sleeping pills, we treat ourselves like some package to be sorted, shipped and delivered. Without time to absorb and to reflect, we leave ourselves reeling, not from adjusting too slowly to a new routine, but from having reached our destination too quickly without ever having the chance to look out of a window. The discomfort, the lag, is of our own making, for all too often, we have arrived without ever having experienced the journey.

Plains Travel

A friend who travelled between Germany and
Johannesburg in the 1950s recounts the excitement of
air travel in those days when planes could not fly at
night. She remembers alighting in Mallorca en route.
All the passengers and crew would go out together for
dinner and dancing and in the morning resume their
journey to the next night's "watering hole," flying over
the desert, passing over herds of wild animals on the
African plains until they finally reached their
destination, refreshed and ready to land. Now she
avoids travel and what she calls being "herded like
cattle."

Perhaps one day we may learn the art of travel again and realize that as we set out, while keeping our destination in mind, we can be grateful if the road is long. There will be no need to hurry the journey, for that is where the adventure and the discovery begin.

5

Place or Time Travel?

The act of vagabonding is not an isolated trend so much as it is a spectral connection between people long separated by place and time, but somehow speaking the same language.

—ROLF POTTS

One's destination is never a place, but a new way of seeing things.

—HENRY MILLER

Even if we stay rooted to the spot, living in the town in which we were born and grew up, we can still long for the exotic, the out-of-our-ordinary. Regardless of where we are, we still travel, for time passes and, though imperceptibly, the earth moves and we with it. Even without changing scenes, each day is a new "home."

If we consider ourselves nomads, each place we "hang our hat" and lay our head becomes our home. From this perspective, we may find ourselves less inclined to think of where we spent last night or what has transpired since we left — and certainly not to consider what is happening there now. Although we carry with us our memories of that place at that time, what we remember no longer exists, whether we stand on the same ground or not.

Perhaps part of our difficulty in coping with the effects of travelling too fast has to do with place rather than time. So tied are we to place, that it is hard to think of "home" as being where we are now and not either where we have come from or where we may find ourselves tomorrow.

Cutting the Grass

On one of my first visits to Sweden, we rented a little cabin by a lake for the weekend. I will always remember my surprise and delight when I saw him outside mowing the lawn. He explained that it needed cutting and that for this weekend, while we lived here, it was our home and our responsibility.

Nomadic existence can bring both a flexibility of world view and a sense of responsibility.

Since time immemorial, Indigenous peoples have considered it their duty, to their ancestors and future generations, to be caretakers for a world that is bigger and wider than the small piece of land on which we, as settlers, live today. Although we think of ourselves as being so firmly rooted in one time and one place, we are inevitably travellers of both.

Salt Songs

The once-nomadic Nuwuvi people are connected through a ceremonial trail passing through four U.S. states, described in the ancient, sacred Salt Songs:

> Besides being indispensable for ritual purposes, Salt Songs and other sacred songs acted as an "oral deed" in the past, marking a family's territory ... With ownership came the responsibility to respect and care for the entire ecology the song encompassed. This ecology not only includes its human occupants, but also the entire ecosystem consisting of flora and fauna, water resources, rocks, mountains, earth, sky, etc., of which they considered themselves caretakers.
>
> —KIM STRINGFELLOW,
> "Bringing Creation Back Together Again"

> One thing our people could not surrender was the meaning of land. In the settler mind, land was property, real estate, capital, or natural resources. But to our people it was everything: identity, the connection to our ancestors, the home of our non-human kinfolk, our pharmacy, our library, the source of all that sustained us. Our lands were where our responsibility to the world was enacted, sacred ground. It belonged to itself; it was a gift, not a commodity, so it could never be bought or sold.
>
> —ROBIN WALL KIMMERER, *Braiding Sweetgrass*

Time and place travel can even be interchangeable when we yearn to leave home on a quest for the unknown, for adventure. Teenagers and young adults living at home with their parents can easily substitute their urge to get away from home with a little homemade time travel. It is perfectly possible to be living in a different time zone from others while living under the same roof. Many teens are able to live at least two if not four time zones away from their parents, only re-joining them at mealtimes when the belly speaks louder than the urge to leave home.

There is part of us all that longs for the freedom of the "open road," the out-of-our-ordinary.

> *There is something in October sets the gypsy*
> *blood astir;*
> *We must rise and follow her,*
> *When from every hill of flame*
> *She calls and calls each vagabond by name.*
> **—WILLIAM BLISS CARMAN, "A Vagabond Song"**

There is gypsy in all of us, yet the word "gypsy" brings images of fortune tellers and beggars, and to call someone a gypsy is considered a racial slur. Like travelling salesmen, tinkers and peddlers, they have ill repute.

> *Somehow it is improper to travel when we work,*
> *as it is improper to work while we travel.*
> **—NELSON H. H. GRABURN,**
> **"Tourism: The Sacred Journey"**

We react with suspicion and mistrust when groups of "travellers" set up camp and move on again when they choose — or when they are asked to leave. Gypsies have long been associated with crime and quackery:

> *My mother said I never should*
> *Play with the gypsies in the wood.*
> *If I did, she would say,*
> *Naughty girl to disobey!*
>
> **—ANONYMOUS**

That old skipping song used to be taught to children as a warning to stay away from "gypsies." A group of colourfully-dressed, dark-skinned outsiders appearing in your village — even if they were there to sell products which had some use or offer specialized services like blacksmithing — caused alarm.

At the same time, as a blogger from New Zealand admits, the song had an appeal:

> *This poem has the allure of the forbidden. It*
> *moves and dances with its own freedom, as it*
> *develops from repression to mystery and new*
> *beginnings.*
>
> **—A.J. PONDER, "My Mother Said...Anonymous"**

The Gypsy at the Door

We would see small groups of Roma women in the town, with babes in arms, selling little posies of heather kept together by tin foil. There wasn't much to distinguish them from others asking for coins, a colourful headscarf perhaps, children beside them looking in need of a meal and a wash, dark eyes sometimes furtive, sometimes world-weary looking into the distance behind and before at a life on the road. In the depths of those eyes I sensed something I also wanted to see, the lure of the unknown, the unimaginable, the exotic. Now and then I'd buy a bunch of lucky heather, as much for the sake of a child as the insistence of her mother that it would bring good fortune.

One day a dark-eyed woman came to the door of our house with a tiny posy and without asking for her palm to be crossed first with any extra silver, she said to my father, "You have a daughter who has been through difficult times. There is a light now at the end of the tunnel." That was a few weeks before he and I met on a beach, both on holiday, living in different countries and brought together by a car stuck in the sand... My father, neither disbelieving what she had said nor inquisitive to hear more, passed on what he had been told. Though curious at the time, it was not until later that I recalled the mystery and the magic of her foretelling.

Romani

The words "Roma" and "Romani" come from the word "Rom," which means "man" in the Romani language. The term "gypsy" comes from the (mistaken) belief that the Romani people originated in Egypt. ... they actually have their roots in India.

The Romani lifestyle has been associated with illegal practices and irregular habits, yet we are fascinated. Part Cherokee, singer Cher, who specialized in lyrics about ethnic discrimination, sung of

> *Gypsies, tramps, and thieves*
> *We'd hear it from the people of the town*
> *They'd call us Gypsies, tramps, and thieves*
> *But every night all the men*
> *would come around*
> *And lay their money down...*
> *to watch the women dance.*
>
> **—CHER, "Gypsies, Tramps, and Thieves"**

Romani music and dance have influenced bolero, jazz and flamenco. There is something elusive about Gypsy music that both beckons us to follow and frightens us in its raw passion. Master teacher and choreographer, Dalia Carella describes her experience of dancing this style:

> *... [A]ll my feelings about those cultures come through my body... I literally lose my own personality and something bigger takes over— something over which I have no control.*

There is an exotic allure to a brightly painted caravan and to following the Romani "happy-go-lucky" way of life:

How could you leave your goose feather bed,
your blankets strewn so comely, oh
how could leave, you've nowhere to go,
all for the raggle taggle gypsy, oh
well what do I care for my goose feather bed
for my blankets strewn comely, oh
to-night I lie in the wide-open field
in the arms of a raggle taggle gypsy, oh
—TRADITIONAL FOLK SONG, "Raggle Taggle Gypsy"

At a distance, gypsies are perceived as exotic, while nearby, they're often seen as

"roving bands of ne'r do wells who lie, steal and
cheat — and play the violin beautifully."
—CRISTEN CONGER, "How Gypsies Work"

Nomadic people the world over have been driven to the fringes of society and sometimes to extinction. With colonization, mass urbanization and organized, state-centric governments, nomadic tribes and cultures have been ostracized for the very fact that they neither "settle down" nor contribute to a sedentary way of life by becoming tax-paying, land-owning citizens. Itinerant communities based on pastoralism rather than land-tenure such as the Irish Travellers, *an lucht siúil*, ("the walking people") are more often considered a problem to the rest of society, travelling from one eviction to the next, rather than a people whose choice to live on the move may have benefits. For once-nomadic Indigenous peoples, taking responsibility for the land that they have travelled since ancient times, has been central to their philosophy of living. As caretakers of land the world over, they have taken seriously their obligations, accepted their dependency and seen the relationship between people and place as an inseparable, interdependent symbiosis.

Is it the obligation we feel to suppress our own craving for freedom and our personal call of the wild that gives the exotic such a forbidden allure? We can feel the attraction of wandering but does the voice of reason or a fear of the unknown bring us back to conform to the familiarity of staying still in the life we know?

Perhaps it is the same call that the Pied Piper played on his flute to entice away the children of Hamelin.

The Wild Woman Archetype

One reason the Gypsy dancer has such a powerful hold on our imagination is that she summons up the archetype of the "wild woman." To an outsider ignorant of Romany culture, the Gypsy seems to live on the edges of civilization, beyond its normal rules. In this romanticized view, the Gypsy dancer appears to be free from societal constraints. The Gypsy as the Wild Woman archetype has magical powers, powers which makes her dangerous. She is out-of-control, or at least beyond the control of the patriarchy. She evokes fear, especially in the subconscious where the Wild Woman lurks within us all. We are afraid to let her out because we may lose control.

—**LAUREL VICTORIA GRAY, "Gypsy in Their Souls"**

6

Bienvenue: *The Enchantment of Arrival*

To be educated is not to arrive,
it is to travel with a different view.

—RICHARD STANLEY PETERS

The traveler sees what he sees.
The tourist sees what he has come to see.

—GILBERT KEITH CHESTERTON

For the very first moments, hours or days in a new place, we look with fresh eyes. We see the small details, take in each sight and sound for the first time. Each new vista stands alone, at face value, without being ranked against how it looked yesterday nor yet invisible as it often becomes when we have grown accustomed to the familiarity of the view.

Finding the Hotel

On Sundays, we often explored and were drawn especially to the mountains, the foothills of the Picos de Europa. Beloved of sailors returning from the New World, those majestic snow-capped peaks were their first sight of home. One Sunday we arrived at a little restaurant called La Xana, in the shadow of a mountain, close to the river, for lunch. The friendly, bustling restaurateur told us what was available on the *Menu del Dia*. Half running, half walking, he prepared and served the meal himself with the assistance of his partner, a slightly built, dark-haired woman who remained in the kitchen. That might have been the end of the story if it had not been for the *trucha con beicon*. One of us discovered after just one bite that it was not good. The restaurateur, concerned about his client's health and perhaps La Xana's reputation, took it upon himself to make sure there had been no ill effects. He knew we lived in a town forty-five minutes away on the coast and assumed that our children were attending the local school there. So, to our surprise, he arrived at the school gates at lunchtime one day later that week. Children generally returned home for a three-course Spanish lunch, so parents would meet and escort their children back for the two-hour break. It was not hard to find us and make his solicitous inquiry about our welfare. His attentiveness impressed us, and during the next months, we became regular clients of La Xana. One day he mentioned the hotel further up the mountain. After lunch we drove up the winding road to see the century-old bakery converted to accommodation. As we passed through the tiny hamlet, over the bridge by the water mill and saw it for the first time, emerging out of the cobbles, we were enchanted. Between ancient oaks and chestnuts trees and a stream overlooked by a little terrace, stood a building that seemed to have grown in situ, welcoming foot-weary travellers and local villagers alike. At the entrance a collection of walking sticks, rough and smooth, short and tall, spoke of distances travelled and those yet to be crossed. Beyond the hotel a well-worn path invited the adventurous further up the mountain to the village above. Over the course of that year, we became the major shareholders of the company running the hotel. We told the restaurateur at La Xana when the trans-actions were complete, and his partner gave a little dance of glee.

La Xana

La Xana is a popular name for businesses throughout Asturias, including restaurants, a brand of local beer, a beauty shop and vacation apartments.

La Xana is a water fairy, a mythological figure thought to be of prehistoric origin, or at the very least, not subject to time as are ordinary humans. Some believe the *Xana* to be a distant memory of a local pre-Christian goddess. Christianity arrived late to Asturias, where a mountainous geography made it possible for large rural populations to practically avoid Romanization and Christianization.

So the old pagan gods receded into the forest, the mountains, the caves, the waterfalls or the sky, sometimes disappearing altogether. However, although they no longer shape everyday action or thought, they still retain their authenticity, occupying a place in popular belief alongside Christianity and modern science. Parish priests have delivered a constant stream of anti-pagan treatises condemning the practitioners of folk traditions, whether medicinal, pagan rite, or cults of local gods as heretics. However, the mythical creatures of Asturias survive in popular tradition. After such demonization, perhaps it is not surprising that in the stories, *Xanas* can be both benevolent — and malicious.

They are usually depicted in one of two ways, the benevolent ones as young beautiful Nordic girls with long blonde hair, and the malicious type as small, thin and dark.

Seeing Through Fresh Eyes

When visitors from other countries came to see us, it was as though we saw all the hidden beauty, the value of village life that we could take for granted at other times. We became tourists in our own home. We saw through their eyes and marvelled at the delights and the unselfconscious charm of rural living. Groups of eight to ten guests travelling from the UK came for a week of guided mountain hikes, and for us their enjoyment of the beauty and the novelty became the amplification of our own. Witnessing and sharing their delight was like reliving our own original wide-eyed wonder magnified, casting and re-casting the spell of our own enchantment.

We can so quickly lose a newcomer's perception, and familiarity can breed not necessarily contempt, but blindness!

It takes time to absorb our surroundings, especially if they are steeped in history. By rushing through, we miss the opportunity to take in everything.

The Temple of Poseidon

When I was twenty-one, visiting Greece for the first time, I felt the compulsion to "see" as much as I could in the short space of a week. Perhaps it was the tourist in me who felt obliged to "make the most" of my short time there, perhaps it was the adventurer looking to do the new and exciting.

On my last day, I boldly hitchhiked to the Temple of Poseidon at Cape Sounion in the unexpected absence of a Sunday bus service. After a short ride with a local resident, a respectful Greek truck driver, I was picked up by a commander who was looking for entertainment on his first day off for three weeks since the American Navy had arrived in Athens Harbour. He didn't know where to go or what to see so relied on the young woman to whom he had given a ride to direct him to a site worthy of a visit and a video.

We arrived, and while I sat on a broken column, just beginning to take in so much history and such beauty, he used his camera to pan 360 degrees. "Ready?" he asked me. I was only ready to sit and absorb. He appeared convinced that he had captured the splendour through the eyes of his camera. Perhaps he expected to carry home the footage to show his family in the comfort of his living room, trying to remember which temple it was or why it had once been important.

Temple of Poseidon
Sounion, Greece

Do we take in "everything" through the lens of a camera? Or do we merely capture a snapshot, or several snapshots, of one place at one time, from an angle which is uniquely our own? One person's "everything" is never the same as someone else's, and while one visitor may look for churches, castles and museums, another may be hearing the variety of birdsong, noticing the different light and its effect on colours or spending time talking with locals to get a feel for what life is like in this new-found world. A tourist, according to Valene Smith, an author and editor of *Hosts and Guests: The Anthropology of Tourism*, is

> *a temporarily leisured person who voluntarily visits a place away from home for the purpose of experiencing change.*

Change includes surprise, the unexpected, whatever that may be, welcome or not, but disappointment and disillusion can only come with preconceived ideas. No amount of reading a guidebook beforehand or looking at the photos of the views after you have left can compare to the experience of being present, then and there, to whatever offers itself to the traveller in the moment. Wonder and awe, amazement — and disbelief — are by-products of this way of seeing.

There is an old Zen saying, "to name the colour is to blind the eye." As soon as we attach words and labels, it becomes easy to stop seeing what is in front of us. When we "collect" experience through the eye of a camera for future viewing, we can be like the student who takes notes, missing the moment, neither here now nor there later, always expecting that we will catch up with ourselves one day... Is it possible instead to be so fully present in the moment as it is happening that the feeling of the memory of that experience will always stand out for us, with neither words, labels nor photos?

We can be tourists guided by expectations or adventurers hungry for the thrill of the chase — or we can travel experiencing change and allowing our travels to change us. The choice is ours, seeing what we have come to see or seeing what we see.

The Language of the Present Tense

One of the things that commends travel, art, nature, work, and certain drugs to us is the way these experiences, at their best, block every mental path forward and back, immersing us in the flow of a present that is literally wonderful—wonder being the by-product of precisely the kind of unencumbered first sight, or virginal noticing, to which the adult brain has closed itself. (It's so inefficient!) Alas, most of the time I inhabit a near-future tense, my psychic thermostat set to a low simmer of anticipation and, too often, worry. The good thing is I'm seldom surprised. The bad thing is I'm seldom surprised.

—MICHAEL POLLAN, *How to Change Your Mind*

7

Perfection, Completion and the Lure of Familiarity

Perfection is achieved, not when there is nothing more to add, but when there is nothing left to take away.

—ANTOINE DE SAINT-EXUPÉRY

Rushing into action, you fail.
Trying to grasp things, you lose them.
Forcing a project to completion,
you ruin what was almost ripe.

Therefore the Master takes action
by letting things take their course.

—LAO TZU

Familiarity breeds contentment.

—GEORGE ADE

The key to enjoying the moment is acceptance and gratitude for where we are, which bring a more acute awareness of the present. But sometimes the temptation to mentally retrace our steps or search for something better loom larger than the place itself. Taking notes about the route for future visits or comparing this to some imagined idea of perfection can detract from our enjoyment of the present.

It can seem to make sense to follow the road, confident that the ideal, that place we have been looking for is around the next corner, but the reality is that it is already here, where we stand, here and now, in this very moment! It becomes easier to stop the unending search for the sublime if we know we have already arrived.

The Perfect Picnic Spot

Travelling in France with my brother and my six-month-old son many years ago proved often to be a hunt for perfection. The "Perfect Picnic Spot syndrome," we called it, because we could drive for hours searching for the one and only, best of all possible picnic spots. First there would be the quest for the right boulangerie for a crusty, warm baguette and the required charcuterie for cheeses and cold meats, perhaps even some *céleri rémoulade* or a portion of finely grated *salade de carottes râpées*. Even a glass of *vin rouge* was not out of the question. But the baby in the backseat became less and less patient. There were times when we reached the right village square only to find that all the shops were closed for lunch.

Then the place to enjoy this feast? Searching for the elusive spot with a crying baby might dampen our delight, but how could we be sure that there was not somewhere even better around the next bend in the road? After finally deciding to stop, there would still be the nagging question — could it have been even more beautiful somewhere else? How could we recognize the perfection of the place because there were probably many more such fields and streams to sit by. We never knew the answer then. Nor can we now.

The pursuit of perfection can become an insatiable quest for the time and the place where everything aligns, obscuring what is around us now. We may realize only in retrospect that the precious, elusive moment has already passed.

The tourist's itch can be addictive, bringing with it a compulsion to see more, do more, in order not to risk missing anything — at least not the sights mentioned in the travel guides. Passing by the signposts for forthcoming attractions and points of interest, the longest, the shortest, the highest, the deepest, the "not to be missed!," can even bring a sense of guilt — "I should have stopped there, seen that, done that." Where do such feelings of obligation come from? Why the need to "be there, do that"? To whom are we answerable when we reach our destination? As far as we know, not even St Peter at the Pearly Gates checks that our passports have the required number of stamps to enter the Kingdom. Fortunately, there is a satiation point, and it's called the *perfection of the present*. When we know that there will never be a moment, in this place, like the one we are experiencing now, we can relinquish the chase for completion. Looking through the eyes of acceptance and curiosity, everywhere is worthy of "sightseeing" from the smallest blade of grass growing valiantly through the concrete to the panoramas that spread before us from mountain tops. The perfect place and time is here and now.

The Perfection of the Present

Recent travels across this vast North American continent took me to a gas-free zone where service stations are a rarity. Not being aware of this important detail, I miscalculated. As I passed some of the most breathtaking, dramatic, and beautiful views of the magnificent shoreline of Lake Superior, my eyes were riveted instead on the gage for the gas tank.

When the needle dropped below thirty kilometres to an unrecordable amount, I decided to pull off the road into a lay-by, not wanting to cause an accident. I searched on my mobile for the nearest filling station but when I attempted to call, I found there was no cell coverage. I tried messaging two sons whom I thought might be able to phone on my behalf, but there was no coverage at all. With only one option left, to flag down a vehicle and seek assistance, I waited a few minutes, bracing myself.

A black truck pulled into the lay-by and, rather than the intimidating truck driver my wary self anticipated, a young couple with a large dog on the back seat became my heroes. I asked them if they could report my predicament to the next gas station they encountered, but after their short walk with Winston, a large, long-haired, gentle giant of a dog, and my own reflections, we agreed that it would be wiser for me to join them on their journey rather than to assume that they would either be believed when they told my story or that someone would be available to travel fifty-four kilometres back to find me.

So, Sheri drove and Jamie and Winston shared the backseat to the next gas station. We compared experiences of driving across the openness of the Prairies and amongst the myriad of lakes of all sizes and shapes that sprinkle Northern Ontario. We discovered that our final destinations on the East Coast were only forty minutes apart. Despite the endless kilometres of pink granite road and the many magical glimpses of the greatest of the Great Lakes, our time together went fast as we exchanged stories of travels and life and delighted in the serendipity of our encounter by the roadside. At the gas station the attendant filled a small red can for me and took it upon himself to ask every customer driving in the direction from which we had come, if they could give me a ride. Overhearing the story of my plight, grandparents with their eleven-year-old granddaughter offered to take me to my car. "It could have happened to us. I hope someone would do the same thing if we were stuck..."

Unlike some travellers who stop to admire those much-anticipated views, my journey was memorable for the unmapped and the unexpected, the realization of an unrepeatable moment — and the generosity of strangers.

Along with the drive to do more, there can also be the compulsion to complete. Perhaps it is a left-over from childhood when we were often told to finish what we had begun, or perhaps it is the desire to be able to say we have been there, done that and can tick it off our list of "must-dos"? There are times when completion seems an arbitrary finish line, dictated by the voice that keeps us on task without heed to the signs along the way that tell us instead to "quit now while the going is good." Completion appears in many guises.

The Wisdom of a Mountain, The Wisdom of a Man

At the age of nineteen, my eldest son Aaron was ready for the expedition of a lifetime. After seven months of intense preparation, he set off to scale the Cerro Aconcagua in Argentina, the highest peak in the world outside Asia. Within 200 metres of the summit, he decided to turn back, and because of this action, discovered a man who had been lost on the mountain for more than 24 hours and saved his life.

Aaron writes in the introduction to his book, *Musicpreneur*, "I began to realize that I had trained only to get to the top and had never visualized my descent..." Like many of us, he found "The hardest part of the decision to turn back was imagining what people back home would think..." But finally, as the summit came into view, he heard the voice of his grandmother who had recently passed away:

"Don't worry about other people," she said. "Making the decision to turn back is harder than deciding to continue. Your friends and family will be proud."

His friends and family are indeed proud and to this day, my son will say that the decision not to complete his mission and the sequence of events that took place afterwards have been some of his "biggest life lessons."

Striving for perfection and completion, even while on holiday, we can drive ourselves to uncomfortable lengths without "time off" to unwind. Sometimes the longing to relax somewhere familiar is greater than the appeal of exploring new ground. Familiarity may breed contempt or blindness — and also offers comfort. Among strangers there is solace when we recognize a familiar, friendly face. It is the lure of the familiar that can take us back time and time again to the same holiday destination where we already know the best beaches, the short cuts, the restaurants where we have become good clients, where to shop, where to hike and when to go. There is satisfaction in knowing your way, even at the cost of overlooking the unexpected, unexplored road.

Without the necessity of having to make choices or decisions, we can rest in the warmth of the known, trust the foreseeable future and bask in the predicable present. For some holidaymakers, setting up home wherever they find themselves is more than a game of "playing house." It provides a welcome certainty and enjoyable familiarity wherever they find themselves.

Travels Across Canada

There were days when I revelled in the opportunity to be transient and anonymous, when I was happy to be able to let go of what was less pleasing, not hold on, just move on in my journey. Savouring the highlights and leaving behind the less appealing sights and sounds with yesterday's travel memories became an easy habit to acquire, an enjoyable disconnection from the familiar attachments of daily life.

There were also days when a continued conversation with a stranger, a second glimpse of a place was welcome, and I watched how quickly my senses recognized and my roots grew towards the known, the personal, the comfortable. Two nights in one spot were enough for me to feel the pull towards people and place:

Days 5 and 6

This two-night stopover in Moosejaw has given me the opportunity to chat with fellow guests at the B&B. Lorraine, twice widowed, commented on how she is repeating her mother's experience of losing two husbands, and I marvel at her resilience, her brave and cheerful spirit. She is not stuck in her losses.

Even to my own surprise, tonight I returned for sushi to the restaurant I visited yesterday. "It must have been very good sushi!" commented a friend who called. It was, but the return for the same experience was the best part, where the waitress knew exactly what I wanted. After studying the menu once again, I asked her for "the same as I had last night, please!" and without hesitation she repeated my order.

Days 8 and 9

While the loons at Black Sturgeon Lake serenaded and the hummingbirds were constantly busy at the feeder among vibrantly coloured flowers, I swam across the lake to an island in water that was as soft as it was warm. A decoy duck greeting me at the dock has fooled many a guest including a Japanese tourist who spent time photographing it, amazed that it did not fly away!

The highlight of my visit to the Log Cabin B&B has been hearing about Deanna's and Tim's strong family ties, despite and because of tragedy, the loss of their youngest son in a skiing accident. When the door of the linen cupboard was open, I caught a glimpse, above the sheets and towels, of cowboy hats lined up on the top shelf, smaller to larger, ready for grandchildren to join their grandparents for a "Cousins' Camp" taking place in two weeks' time. This year the theme is "cowboys." Children four years and above can participate and parents are not included. No wonder that there is a sign at the entrance of the Log Cabin: "Grandmother's House where Cousins become Friends." The warmth of their hospitality assures all who enter that they will be welcomed here.

The Log Cabin B&B

Mapping my route and booking my bed before I started my cross-Canada journey, I was attracted by the Treadways' story of courage and strength which I read about on the website for the Log Cabin B&B. They were one of two couples chosen to spend a year in the Manitoba prairies, living like the pioneers of 1875. Their experience was documented on History Channel and National Geographic in a television series called *Pioneer Quest: A Year in the Real West*:

> "They suffered ill health, barn burning, mosquitoes, desperate loneliness, coldest December in 120 years, BUT they reaped peacefulness & a serenity that comes from a slower pace of life."
>
> **—DEANNA AND TIM TREADWAY, "About the Innkeepers"**

Days 16 and 17

Two nights at The Orange Bicycle B&B in Tobermory
where Neda and Nick have treated me like family: "Can
we adopt you?" they asked. "You are adorable!" So are
they. So many great stories out on the terrace where
they invited me to join other guests for wine one
evening and where they brought out their coffee mugs
and took turns standing to talk while serving us
sumptuous breakfasts. A wonderful swim in cool clear
waters at Little Cove, on the rocky shores of Lake
Huron, with my left-over breakfast as a snack, kindly
packed by Neda...

The Orange Bicycle

Neda, originally from Tehran, had to sell her bicycle when she was fifteen because girls were no longer allowed to ride bicycles after the Islamic Revolution in Iran. After emigrating to Canada in 1998, she purchased a secondhand bicycle in Kensington Market and a few months later got a job as a bike courier in downtown Toronto. When Nick bought her another one, it was time to retire her old bicycle. Neda decided to keep the Huffy, her first Canadian bike and loyal partner, and planted it in their backyard. In their next house the bike was spray-painted orange and promoted to the front garden. When Nick and Neda moved to Tobermory, the orange bicycle went with them and was given a position of honour in the front garden where it shares the cheerfulness of its bright presence with all who pass by!

> "We love to travel, to meet new friends, to share cultural values, to respect our differences and promote peace and love, to laugh and not take ourselves too seriously. We love to share our beautiful home with you. Bringing one smile at a time to everyone's face is our mission.
>
> Be happy, N&N"
>
> **—NICK AND NEDA, "About Us"**

Travel provides the opportunity to move back and forth between the personal and the impersonal. My focus alternates between looking within at my life as I live it in this world, to looking without at other people in other places living theirs. I gain some perspective and see the universal nature of life as it is lived in countless ways. Each of the people I meet on my journey is a unique manifestatios of the common thread that unites us all, wherever we live, whatever the life we lead. All that counts is this same energy that flows through and animates us all — and how we make use of it.

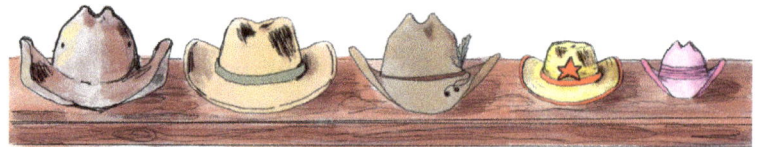

The Significance of Insignificance

As I rested on a rock in the morning, the sun emerged over the horizon, casting a giant shadow of the Aconcagua over the surrounding mountains. I distinctly remember it because it looked like a giant pyramid with the sun directly at its peak. At that moment I remember feeling totally insignificant in the grand scheme of things. Material objects had absolutely no importance. I felt small and the world felt immense. I was grateful for the oxygen I was breathing and became acutely aware of what was truly valuable... I felt truly humbled at the enormity of the world and of life. I was a small being among massive and majestic mountains.

—**AARON BETHUNE,** *Musicpreneur*

8

Pan Del Dia:
The Currency of Language and the Language of Currency

What we have forgotten is that thoughts and words are conventions... A convention is a social convenience, as, for example, money ... but it is absurd to take money too seriously, to confuse it with real wealth ... In somewhat the same way, thoughts, ideas and words are "coins" for real things.

—ALAN WATTS

If a word is worth a coin, silence is worth two.

—HEBREW PROVERB

Words and coins are symbols. Words refer to a familiar object or concept. When spoken, after many repetitions, the sound becomes recognizable, and when written, in the form of a collection of hieroglyphics called letters, we learn to understand what they represent. Coins stand for the value of the gold once stored in world banks. With translator apps and foreign exchange values given in an instant, it is easy to forget that both language and currency stand for something beyond their "face value."

WORDS

Language, some might say, is no more than a taste on the tongue in passing, the sound in the ears as spoken, or the sight on the page, drawn left to right or up and down, depending on what part of the world you are from. Its function is a means to an end, to communicate.

Learning Language Through Osmosis

When we first moved to Spain, I spoke little Spanish and what I learnt was mainly through osmosis, a process of absorbing the meaning before I could imitate the sound myself, just as a child understands what is being said long before he or she can talk coherently. Whole expressions still come to me with no clue as to how the words are spelled nor do I search for the equivalent expression in English. Without directly translating by using a dictionary, there grows an awareness of when something fits the context which may be quite different from the comparable situation in our familiar mother tongue. The result is my inter-mittent, incomplete Spanish, imperfectly present, sprinkled with whole expressions that emerge fully formed on a bed of hesitant word-hunting attempts to achieve communication. Initially my vocabulary, such as it was, was mainly *verduras* (vegetables) since I learnt through grocery shopping and my teacher was "the bread lady" who kindly corrected me whenever opportunity permitted. The method of instruction was the language of smiles and laughter and the reward for learning was the loaf of a *pan rustico* still warm from the oven...

Who would not learn in that currency? No wonder that to this day both hearing and speaking Spanish bring me joy.

There is more to language than the words that meet the ear. Body language, intonation, the feeling behind and the silence between the words are also communication that changes according to the culture, the situation, the speakers and the listeners. The message between the written lines can speak more loudly than the words. Language itself has evolved with the speakers. Perhaps getting to the point quickly with a clipped phrase, parting with words more reluctantly, suits a colder climate because opening one's mouth is an action exercised frugally and with caution? Similarly, the more expansive painting with words of the Latin languages, often accompanied by gesticulations, is more comfortably afforded in warmer temperatures. Different languages seem to express certain ideas and concepts more clearly, some lend themselves to scientific examination and others identify the subtle difference between definitions, untranslatable to another tongue. Behind all of it though is the human expression we hear and recognize intuitively, no matter the words, no matter the language. Words are the brush strokes painted on the white page of silence as we reach out to one another. Communication includes it all — the colour of the paint, the sweep of the stroke and the backdrop of the canvas.

Behind the sound, we can listen to the feeling. Translations and definitions become meaningless in the art of communication if we fail to hear the tone and the intent. If we listen to words as though we are listening to music, the silence between the sounds becomes as important as the words themselves.

Jimi Hendrix

On the same visit to Greece mentioned in an earlier chapter, I ventured to travel to Hydra, one of the Greek islands. Behind the marketplace with its little picture-postcard harbour and booths for selling souvenirs to eager tourists, there was a path around the mountain, away from the photogenic "stage-front" to where the local people gathered their goats. A young man approached me:

"Ameri-can?"

"No."

"Speak Engleesh?"

"Yes!"

With arms waving to indicate flight and a look of horror on his face he explained:

"Athena aerodromio. Bang bang! Jimi Hendrix!"

By his urgent tone, I recognized his panic, shock and alarm. It was 5th August 1973, the day that two Arab gunmen hurled grenades and fired machine guns, killing three people and wounding fifty-five in the crowded transit lounge of the Athens airport. From this brief communication, I knew in an inexplicable flash that there had been a shooting at the airport and some people were dead, like "Jimi Hendrix," no doubt the first dead American to come to mind for this young man. He felt he needed to warn me and to reach out to another human being to express his distress.

This same young man, inquiring whether I had anywhere to stay that night introduced me to his landlady who had a hostel where she offered basic sleeping arrangements to the visitors passing through — one room for women and one for men, simple and sufficient.

When we make an effort to speak someone else's language, however imperfect our attempt, we convey our willingness to take a risk as well as our desire to communicate. Being comfortable to make a mistake, to be corrected, sometimes to be the cause of laughter and to be a ready student no matter what, tells the listener more about us than any words alone can do. Speaking more slowly, enunciating with care instead of increasing your volume as though the listener is deaf, indicates patience, persistence and the ability to put ourselves in their shoes as they attempt to understand someone valiantly mutilating and distorting their language.

Language is empty and meaningless, no matter what it represents, if it is simply the translation found in the dictionary. It can sometimes be misleading to read only the disembodied words in their stark lettered nakedness. Words are the pegs on which we hang the objects and concepts we wish to point to and whether consciously or not we also communicate the feeling with which they are delivered.

> *Everyday speech is ... a case of shared improvisation. You meet someone new and you create language together. There is a commerce of feeling and information back and forth, exquisitely coordinated. When conversation works, it is ... not a matter of meeting halfway. It is a matter of developing something new to both of us.*
> **—STEPHEN NACHMANOVITCH, *Free Play***

Does the Language We Speak Influence How We Communicate?

Countries that speak the Romance languages (French, Italian, Spanish and Portuguese) and Latin American countries have "higher context" cultures, meaning that communication relies on a greater number of non-verbal cues and covert messages than in "lower" context cultures. There are more words that can be interpreted multiple ways depending on how and when they are used. High-context languages tend to be spoken in countries with a long history so that meaning becomes implicit and is passed on for generations. Japan, an island nation with thousands of years of shared language and culture, is the highest context culture in the world.

"Low-context" languages are those in which the meaning is made explicit. English is the lowest context language and the United States is the lowest context culture.

Countries with greater cultural diversity in the population and less shared history tend to have a lower context culture.

What is the Impact of These Differences?

If you are from a low-context culture you might assume that someone from a higher context culture is secretive, unable to communicate — even untrustworthy! If you speak a high-context language then you may find that people from a low-context culture tend to state the obvious, sound condescending — even patronizing!

> There are seven times more words in English than in French (500,000 versus 70,000), ... Many words in French have multiple possible meanings... which means that the listener is responsible for discerning the intention of the speaker.
>
> **—ERIN MEYER,** *The Culture Map*

Kuuki wo Yomu

Kuuki wo yomu, "reading the air," is a Japanese custom similar to the Western phrase "reading between the lines." It means to be situationally aware and attentive to the thoughts, feelings, and needs of the people around you without the need for verbal expression. ("KY" means not "reading the air.") When you are in Japan you may read the air in order not to insult anyone, but it is always helpful to be situationally aware. The air changes far more quickly and imperceptibly than the paper on which the lines are written...

Does the Language We Use Influence Our Perceptions?

Language is often used metaphorically, almost without our awareness.

Swedish and English speakers, for example, tend to think of time in terms of distance — "What a *long* day!" Spanish and Greek speakers, on the other hand, tend to think of time in terms of volume — "What a *full* day!" According to a study, the difference between thinking of time as a distance to cross, or a container to be filled, affects the thinker's perception of the passage of time.

Living Language

The language we use influences our perceptions in so many subtle but significant ways. My first experience of gender applied to inanimate objects was in early French lessons where suddenly a previously flat observation about "my aunt's pen" could be transformed to "*la plume de ma tante.*" The pen was not only given importance, mentioned before my aunt, but also became instantly fluid, flowing and feminine, filled with possibility, quite unlike "my aunt's pen," or for that matter, "*le pupitre,*" the desk, which remained a solid and inflexible block behind which you were often forced to sit for too long. The assignment of gender to an otherwise lifeless object opens up a world of invisible nuances and possibilities.

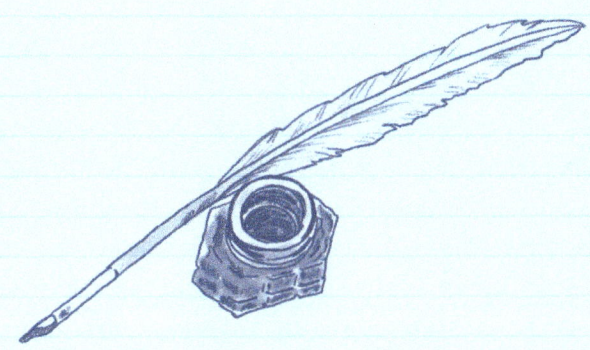

Grammatical gender, used in a quarter of the world's languages seems to have grown as a convenient way of classifying nouns and the agreement of their associated articles, adjectives and prepositions to avoid ambiguities. This has been lost in the English language and we often require repetition of the noun in a sentence to avoid confusion. In some languages grammatical gender, the choice of a particular verb, or the use of a verb rather than a noun, also indicate whether an object is animate or inanimate.

To be a hill, to be a sandy beach, to be a
Saturday, all are possible verbs in a world where
everything is alive. Water, land and even a day,
the language a mirror for seeing the animacy of
the world, the life that pulses through all things...
—ROBIN WALL KIMMERER, *Braiding Sweetgrass*

Although language grows over time for the convenience of its native speakers, it also reflects a difference in world views that shapes new speakers, listeners and writers. When we classify what may otherwise appear to be lifeless objects as either feminine or masculine, we acknowledge, if even imperceptibly, a quality of aliveness in them. This changes everything as it demonstrates respect for other beings whether or not they appear to be alive in our limited view of what that means. We attribute the highest order of animacy to human beings and often assume that along with sentient awareness, we also have the unique capability to impact our world. When we acknowledge other life forms apart from our own, we open the way for consideration of *their* agency, their ability to have effect on the environment. We recognize the possibility that there is one life force that flows through everything, at whatever point it is in the continuum of animation. Grammatical gender recognizes such a current of animacy.

There is an opportunity in speaking more than one language to try out different "costumes," different ways of being in and seeing the world. Learning other languages gives a key to opening many new doors in understanding.

COINS

Coins and paper money have only face value, no matter their appearance, the weight of the coins or the pictures of the monarchs which grace the paper version of a "promise to pay the bearer." Once, a bill indicated the amount of gold bullion it represented. Now, though the cost to produce a banknote is minimal, its real value lies in the value of the goods and services for which it can be exchanged. No amount of coins, bills or even gold would be of any use on a desert island. As economist Milton Friedman puts it, "the pieces of green paper have value because everybody thinks they have value."

Coins and bills have worth which varies in subtle ways, unrecorded by exchange rates and the apps that provide instant figures on a screen, even without the phenomenon of devaluation or the printing of new bills. There is a currency that lives between the lines of the goods and services money buys which alters more slowly than the daily fluctuations of the exchange rate and cannot be so easily measured. Although buying a fresh loaf of bread every day may seem like an extravagance in North America, in many European countries it is considered a priority, a ritual that is worth far more than the Euros it costs to buy. The bread is different, the flour is different and most of all, the respect with which it is regarded gives it an importance in daily life unmeasured by the coins required for its purchase.

What we choose to spend money on is far more important than the value of the money itself. It is how we vote, how we show our support for small businesses or large corporations. When we are on holiday, we are also showing our allegiance to one destination or another, one type of tourism or another and paving the way for those who may follow in our footsteps.

Banking with Royalty

Parmigiano-Reggiano, often called Parmesan cheese, is an edible currency known as "The King of Cheeses." Italian bank Credito Emiliano, or "Credem" as it is known locally, has been accepting the cheese as collateral from farmers needing a personal loan since 1953. If the farmers default on the loan, then the bank sells the cheese and these golden wheels can be worth thousands of dollars. The bank's climate-controlled vaults, containing up to 430,000 cheeses valued at $187 million, has been hit by bank-robbers three times, most recently in 2009. Were they looking for the cheese — or the "cheese," you might ask!

Pan del Dia

A Dutch friend who had spent years travelling with the circus, told us how when they arrived at a new village, they would be able to predict the success of their performance, the welcome the circus would receive, by the taste of a loaf of freshly-baked bread from the local *panadería*.

A young man working for us one summer was given the rather mindless task of catching up with the pile of invoices that had mounted up over several months. Instead of working chronologically from the oldest, he began with the most recent. With a methodical mindset I was curious to know why he began with the most recent, working backwards instead of starting with the oldest and working forwards. He told me, "If you don't eat the *pan del dia* today, you will never taste fresh bread and will always be catching up with yesterday's leftovers." He knew about enjoying the moment and how living and working in the present also helps us to look after yesterday's backlog more efficiently. Take care of those pennies of the present and the pounds of the accumulated past seem better able to take care of themselves.

The value of coins and words lies in where they point us, what they represent and how we employ them. In themselves, however delightful their appearance or sweet their sound, they are metaphors. While coins can assume a value on which empires are built, like castles in the air, words too weave their magic spells in poetry, prose and in the letters of calligraphy, taking on layers of meaning beyond their pragmatic function of communication.

With both currency and language we are reminded that we have the freedom to choose which goods or services to buy, which interpretation or translation to use — how to communicate what matters to us. Between the words, between the coins, there lies an invisible truth, there for us to discover if we listen beyond appearances and "read the air."

9

Guidebooks, Maps and Getting Lost

Traveler, there is no path;
paths are made by walking.

—ANTONIO MACHADO

The "path" comes into existence
only when we observe it.

—WERNER HEISENBERG

As you start to walk on the way,
the way appears.

—JALĀL AL-DĪN MUḤAMMAD RŪMĪ

GUIDEBOOKS

Guidebooks are suggestions, pointing towards a direction without telling us which way to go or insisting that we go there. The choice is ours, direct route, scenic route or bypass. Coach tours and cruises on the other hand, for the most part, are based on decisions already made for us and organized behind the scenes, representing for some an easy way to see the world without the research beforehand or during a holiday. Places change over time and prices often rise, so travel guides have to be updated regularly.

The First Guidebook

The *Codex Calixtinus* is a twelfth-century illuminated manuscript, originally attributed to Pope Callixtus II. Chapter 5 of the eleven chapters, the *Iter pro peregrinis ad Compostellam* is a comprehensive guide describing the French route for pilgrims journeying to Santiago de Compostela in northern Spain. The author, who seems more likely to have been a French monk, reviews the days' journeys, hostels, natural accidents that cross the route, the city of Santiago of Compostela, the cathedral and other churches in the capital of Galicia.

He talks about the customs of the towns and cities and the shrines that the pilgrim should not miss. He also includes a series of practical tips for travellers and warnings about the dangers they might encounter on their adventure to Compostela. He includes anecdotes from his own journey and his views on the barbaric customs of local inhabitants. Notable among these reflections is his impression of the people of northern Spain whom he describes as "fierce-faced men who terrorize people with their barbarian tongues." He speaks of the Basque people and those from Navarre as being "full of evil, dark in complexion, of aberrant appearance, wicked, treacherous, disloyal and false." He accuses them of being thieves and murderers who "eat, drink and dress like pigs" and in particular, complains about the food. He encourages readers not to try "the fish that the vulgar call catfish" because according to him, those who ingest it run the risk of "being sick."

The competition between French *haute-cuisine* and Spanish *gastronomia* is long-standing!

MAPS

We represent reality with maps and nautical charts in order to make sense of the intricacies of our world. A map, like a language, can then appear to us more real than the land it represents, despite the fact that, as pointed out by Alfred Korzybski in *Science and Sanity*, "a map is not the territory," just as words are themselves not more than symbols.

So keen we are to grasp a picture of our world that we will go to any lengths to reduce reality to two dimensions or at best a three-dimensional raised relief map. Even a map using a scale of a mile to a mile would only be a representation.

Some of us only resort to unfolding a ragged rendering of the terrain once we are already lost, somewhat similar to reading the instructions when all else has failed.

Terra Cognita

In the *Hereford Mappa Mundi* [c.1300], the Garden of Eden is located at the top of the map in an island at the eastern extreme of the world. The map displays the inhabited part of the world, as much of it as was known then, equivalent to Europe, Asia and North Africa, seen through the lens of Christian Europe with Jerusalem at the centre. As more "*terra incognita*" was "discovered," religious map-makers had to shift the location of Paradise. By the time of the *Catalan-Estense Map* of 1450, the Garden had been moved to Ethiopia, presumably because Marco Polo had not found it in Asia.

In Lewis Carroll's *Sylvie and Bruno Concluded* (1893), a mysterious character, Mein Herr, announces that "we actually made a map of the country, on a scale of *a mile to the mile!*" When asked if the map has been used much, Mein Herr admits,

> "It has never been spread out, yet. The farmers objected: they said it would cover the whole country and shut out the sunlight! So we now use the country itself, as its own map, and I assure you it does nearly as well."
>
> **—LEWIS CARROLL**

If we consider that our personal view of the world is only a description of reality as *we* see it and that each person's "map" is of their own creating, we might agree with Mein Herr, that the "country" we see makes a good map. After all, as Alfred Korzybski observed, it is still, at best, only a representation and not the territory.

On the other hand, maps can be shared orally. Such maps are adaptable, flexible, informative, living chronicles of space and time, uniting those who have already travelled with those about to set out on their journeys. The ancient sacred Salt Songs of the once-nomadic Nuwuvi people is a map shared through song. It is both a chart of their ancestral territories and a guidebook for the ceremonial trail that spans across the Mojave Desert, the southern Great Basin, the northwestern Colorado Plateau and the north-central Colorado Desert. The 142 Salt Song cycle brings together the sacred places in a long, continuous loop, describing locations of ancient villages, places to gather life-giving salt, medicinal herbs, foodstuffs, trade routes, sacred sites and other important geographical features that were in the past necessary for their continued survival. In addition, when sung during private memorials and other sacred ceremonies today, Salt Songs encourage community healing by connecting contemporary Nuwuvi to their ancestors and the landscape they once inhabited, a three-dimensional map of space and time, uniting people, place, and story.

GLOBAL POSITIONING SYSTEMS (GPS)

Nowadays, thanks to GPS systems, we can receive directions which are usually correct and often delivered by an imperturbable robotic voice. Fresh instructions follow each time we choose a different destination. A GPS has the ability to adjust instantly and repeatedly to a new route, a new location or even to a new task master. A calm and patient GPS system will take change in stride, remaining unflustered by road works, floods and other detours and never tires of recalculating in real time where we are at this moment. Like the signage at a park which tells you, "You are here" on the map so that you can calculate which way to go, the GPS reminds you that you are already here and that "if you've no destination, you've already arrived."

Travels with Samantha

Samantha is my travelling companion for this journey from the west to the east coast of Canada. Calm, and patient, she is ever ready to re-calculate our bearings when I, the driver, have gone astray. Sometimes she seems too quiet, only speaking up when I have taken the wrong turn or when finally, there are some instructions to give. It's then that I wish she was more communicative — perhaps a word or two here and there about the local history or even the latest score in the baseball game. Passing a remark about the weather wouldn't be bad, just now and again, or telling me that I am still on the right track when the hum of the road seems to go on forever. But she asks for nothing and seems as dispassionate when I go the wrong way as she is unpraising when I follow her directions to the letter.

She has come to my rescue a few times and her level-headedness more than makes up for her reticence. Sometimes however, when she gets it wrong, she can stick stubbornly to her idea of where we should go, even when roadwork has forced our route to change. She announced to me the other day that I was driving in the wrong direction on a one-way lane, not realizing that traffic had been diverted from a four-lane highway to allow for construction.

There have been times too when she has insisted that my destination is a private house and not the B&B where I am booked for the night. On occasions like that I overrule her, relying on my inner compass and common sense rather than her obstinate resistance to change and inflexibility of ideas. Still, there are no hard feelings, and she is always back in the map-reader's seat in the morning, ready to start the day afresh with no complaints about my reluctance to follow her recommendations the previous day. There is a growing loyalty between us, the trust that comes with familiarity.

What is GPS and how does it work?

The GPS is a navigation system using satellites, a receiver and algorithms to synchronize location, velocity and time data for air, sea and land travel.

The satellite system consists of a constellation of twenty-four satellites in six Earth-centred orbital planes, each with four satellites, orbiting at 13,000 miles (20,000 km) above Earth and travelling at a speed of 8,700 mph (14,000 km/h).

While we only need three satellites to produce a location on Earth's surface, a fourth satellite is often used to validate the information from the other three. The fourth satellite also allows us to calculate the altitude of a device.

COMPASSES

Modern navigation relies on a globally integrated system in which each voyage from start to finish is concerned with four basic objectives: staying on course, avoiding collisions, minimizing fuel consumption, and conforming to an established timetable.

Compasses are valuable navigation tools for sailors and for hikers as well. If all else fails, the compass will tell you in which direction you are looking. Then, if you know where you want to travel and choose to stay your course, you can at least head the right way. It cannot tell you where you are, like a GPS, or suggest how you may get to where you want to go, like a travel guide. Still, it has the advantage of being able to let you know which way it is pointing, so that if you are facing the same way, with the aid of a map and the recognition of some landmarks, you have a chance of finding your path. Not so at sea when you are out of sight of land, hence the need for further instruments and extensive calculations that will take into consideration both time and place. Nowadays the binnacle on a ship's bridge includes a sextant for celestial navigation, a compass and chart for marine orienteering, a chronometer to give the time accurately and a marine GPS.

Deviation

If you were using a compass 800,000 years ago and facing north, the needle would point to the south magnetic pole. Why? Even though the Earth acts like a giant magnet, it is not stable. Both the north and south magnetic poles are slowly shifting. Since the magnetic North Pole was discovered in the early nineteenth century, it has drifted northward by more than 966 kilometres (600 miles) and it continues to move about 40 miles per year. The north and south magnetic poles have also switched places many times in the Earth's history.

Chronometers: Location in Place Through Time

A chronometer determines longitude by comparing the local time with the reading of a clock that reliably keeps the time of a known meridian. Because the Earth revolves 360° in 24 hours, or $1/4$° every minute, it is possible to determine how far east or west a ship has travelled by comparing a marine timekeeper set to keep time with the location of the ship's point of departure and the ship's local time as measured by the Sun and stars with a sextant.

"The Only Constant Is Change" — Heraclitus

Shakespeare's Julius Caesar insists, "But I am constant as the Northern Star, of whose true fixed and resting quality there is no fellow in the firmament." According to Kenneth Chang, writing in the *New York Times*, Caesar should have said "fickle as the Northern Star." Polaris, the current North Star, appearing over the North Pole, is a *cepheid variable*, a pulsating star that brightens and dims periodically because of the expansion and contraction of helium gas in its outer layers. Over time, even its pulsations have been changing, slowing down so that the period of oscillation lengthens eight seconds a year...

Due to the cyclical wobble of Earth's rotational axis, even the northness of Polaris is changeable. In ancient Egypt, another star, Thuban, was the North Star. Over time, as Earth's axis tipped, Thuban appeared to move away, and Polaris to approach the pole. When Shakespeare wrote those lines in the play, Polaris was still close enough to be considered the North Star, though farther from the pole than it is now.

However, in Caesar's time, the first century BC, there was no "true fixed" North Star so these famous Shakespearean lines are an "astronomical anachronism."

"CODDIWOMPLING"

Not all those who wander are lost.

—J.R.R. TOLKEIN

Although "coddiwompling" may fall short of the practical way-finding systems mentioned earlier, it can be an invaluable guide in setting a course in the first place. The four basic objectives of modern navigation: "staying on course, avoiding collisions, minimizing fuel consumption, and conforming to an established timetable" are all dependent on knowing first where we want to go and how we want to get there. Or we may have chosen a destination and have already arrived, but how do we want to spend our time and make the most of a break from familiar routine? Coddiwompling, "travelling in a purposeful manner towards a vague destination" is an English (slang) term, similar to the French word *dérive*, a drift or an unplanned journey in which participants drop their everyday relations and "let themselves be drawn by the attractions of the terrain and the encounters they find there." This may be the secret to a *trouvaille*, a discovery, the French word for "a chance encounter with something wonderful" that is more likely to take place when we are free of expectations and open to serendipity and synchronicity:

> *I travel with a purpose. My purpose is to adventure, have fun, laugh, explore, learn, try new things and meet new people. Mostly, in places where I have no idea what to expect....*

Sometimes in travel and life, expectations can be
the very thing that destroy an incredible place, a
moment, even a memory.

—"The Adventure Diary"

According to CNN Travel, travel makes us happy because
it promises us the opportunity for self-discovery:

> *experiential travel is about presenting the*
> *customer with the surprise of the "unknown," the*
> *luxury of "unexpected choices" and the*
> *empowerment of "overcoming hurdles" (such as*
> *scaling a peak) so that he feels he has completed*
> *a "journey towards self-actualization."*

Those magical moments of unexpected, unsolicited
adventures often lead to personal growth and become the
"stuff" that memories are made of.

> *A walk, following your intuitive promptings, down*
> *the streets of a foreign city holds rewards far*
> *beyond a planned tour of the tried and tested....*
> *When you travel in this way you are free; there are*
> *no have-to's and shoulds. You are structured at*
> *first only, perhaps, by the date of the plane*
> *departure. As the pattern of people and places*
> *unfolds, the trip, like an improvised piece of music,*
> *reveals its own inner structure and rhythm.*

—STEPHEN NACHMANOVITCH, *Free Play*

Las Cuevas de Llonin

On one of our hikes with visitors from the UK we were walking through a village, which was at one time known for cheesemaking. The traditional blue cheeses were aged in caves, but in this village the caves had been closed for entry by anyone for some years. We wandered past and noticed the metal gate to seal it off from unwanted explorers was open, so rather than sticking to our itinerary, we cautiously entered to find out what was happening. To our amazement and delight, and that of our guests, we found a party of archeologists and geologists within, testing and photographing what was inside. We were given a tour by an enthusiastic professor who explained how they had found evidence of the use of lower levels of the cave as a den for hyenas and leopards and higher levels where human artifacts had been uncovered. We saw prehistoric engravings and paintings of deer, reindeer horns, goats, snakes and a bison, the best example of Paleolithic art in the region, created 12,000–33,000 BP (Before Present).

The caves had been closed to cheesemaking for some time as the cheese was destroying the paintings. Although there is a replica of the art on display elsewhere, this and other similar well-known paintings seventy kilometres away are no longer viewable in case they too are destroyed by the moisture generated by human breath.

GETTING LOST

*It may be that when we no longer know what to
do we have come to our real work, and that when
we no longer know which way to go we have come
to our real journey.*

—WENDELL BERRY, *Standing by Words*

This chapter would not be complete without a few words
about getting lost. Getting lost can provide the opportunity to discover things you didn't know you were looking
for. Since losing your way is a more common experience
when you are travelling in unfamiliar places, it seems
worth mentioning the benefits when the disadvantages
can be all too obvious. We all experience loss in one form
or another at some point in our lives. It is an inevitable
part of human experience, so having a little practice in
handling the unknown, the unsolicited and often the
unwelcome, is useful.

Generally speaking, we become more aware of our
surroundings when we are lost — in order to find our
bearings. Everything else has to wait.

*It is an ironic habit of human beings to run faster
when we have lost our way.*

—ROLLO MAY, *Love and Will*

But if we don't panic and don't run faster, perhaps in
the wrong direction, we tend to be hyper-present and
acutely aware of the smallest detail, discovering surprises
we had no idea were there. The challenge of finding the
way also increases our self-awareness, creativity, and

problem-solving abilities. Asking for directions can be an exercise in humility and finding the right way again, a point of pride, reassuring us that we are indeed self-reliant, resourceful and resilient.

Catching the Bus

Many years ago I travelled across France with two companions. With somewhat of a youthful spirit of adventure, we lost our way, and spying a bus with the name of the town we were looking for on its destination indicator, we decided to follow it — right into the bus station where it was parking after its last journey of the day. Such an adventure is now a source of amusement. Any sense of frustration or impatience at the time has long since evaporated.

San Sebastian de Garandal

On another occasion we were driving, as we often did on Sundays, just to explore. I had given our eldest son the task of map-reading so that he could practice such a useful skill by directing me, the driver, where to go without the concern or consequence of arriving anywhere late. Although his first attempts took us further and further into "terra incognita," we were curious and had the time to find out what was at the end of the narrow winding road we were ascending behind coachloads of sightseers. To our surprise we found the buses parked in the little village square and hordes of people climbing the steep path to the pine trees above the village. Many of the Sunday tourists looked as though such a hike could be their last, and they were clearly not prepared for such exertion. We soon realized that we had come upon a religious gathering. Crowds of people were standing around more than one prostrate body, fervently praying. It was the little village where miracles were recorded in the 1960s, where four 10- to 11-year-old-girls, apparently guided solely by what they were experiencing, engaged in "ecstatic walks or ambulatory ecstasy," including countless "conversations" with the Archangel Michael and the Virgin Mary. They would walk throughout the village, up and down stairways and in and out of homes, at all hours of the day.

Very often they ran at great speed down the precipitous mountainside, even backward — so swiftly that even the young men of the village running at top speed could not keep up...

Even following buses can lead to unexpected destinations and unsolicited adventures which we remember far longer than the times when we have known where we are going.

There is also the matter of "losing oneself," because of course, in some ways, going on holiday is just that, a way to lose one's familiar self:

> *To be lost is to be fully present, and to be fully*
> *present is to be capable of being in uncertainty*
> *and mystery. And one does not get lost but loses*
> *oneself, with the implication that it is a conscious*
> *choice, a chosen surrender, a psychic state*
> *achievable through geography.*
> **—REBECCA SOLNIT, *A Field Guide to Getting Lost***

Here is where the difference lies between losing one's way and losing oneself, a goal which may be more challenging than simply not finding the way. One depends on a certain ignorance, even a clumsiness, and the other is a perhaps unconscious choice or an intentional attempt at shedding the familiar self among unfamiliar surroundings.

Losing Himself

We were in Ibiza overnight en route from Valencia. We had finished our meal, sitting still, heavy with the day's journey, outside under the trees of a small square, only the streetlights to see by. The music was everywhere, groups of partygoers and clubbers unaware that their voices were becoming louder as the drinks flowed. Ibiza, famous for its wild nightlife was our stop for a night's sleep before we continued onwards the next day. A new song began, and as if called by the Pied Piper, our youngest son, perhaps five or six at the time, awoke and arose. Dusty and dishevelled from the long travels, he strayed to the centre of the square as if it were a stage and began to move to the music. With total absorption in his dance, he seemed oblivious of the fact that a small group of adults were watching his every unchoreographed step. While the partygoers were intentionally losing themselves in alcohol, a little boy became the sounds he could feel through each fibre of his small body, expressing the music without a whisper of self.

> *Not till we are lost, in other words not till we have lost the world, do we begin to find ourselves, and realize where we are and the infinite extent of our relations.*
>
> **—Henry David Thoreau, *Walden***

10

Mono No Aware:
The Beauty of Transience

I was born under a wandrin' star
Wheels are made for rolling,
mules are made to pack
I've never seen a sight that
didn't look better looking back
I was born under a wandrin' star

—ALAN LERNER AND FREDERICK LOEWE

Take only memories; leave only footprints.

—CHIEF SEATTLE

J ars of preserved holiday memories can be opened at will when the situation requires — in times of stress or in happy recall when basking in nostalgia.

Planning in advance to capture such moments, or intentionally creating the circumstances which promote their occurrence, seems impossible because those occasions we most enjoy remembering are often the most unexpected and spontaneous. But like the jars of jam made sweet from berries ripened in summer sunshine, or the vintage year for wine, stored memories also depend on both local conditions and our own skills as gardeners and vintners. By better knowing ourselves and our companions, we can ensure, to the best of our abilities, the conditions for making joy-filled memories. And if happy occasions depend on an element of serendipity then, as Louis Pasteur pointed out,

chance favours only the prepared mind.

We can store these cherished memories for recollection and reliving, savouring the magic of a time that has passed. It is worth considering beforehand how we might fill those jars and bottles when we are in the midst of planning and planting the seeds for a holiday.

Making Memories

"Have a good holiday!" When we were about to leave on the journey of a lifetime, our emigration to Canada, we first went on a family vacation, driving, all five of us in the car, to the south of France. A friend wished us a good holiday, telling us to "make happy memories!" At the time, I wondered how it could be possible to set off with the intention, ahead of time, of consciously making memories of any kind.

Holiday Windows

My grandfather took up painting, something he had always wanted to do, when he was sixty. He and my grandmother spent many happy holidays after that, usually on coach trips to beautiful locations where he would take out his easel and paints, unfold his artist's stool and paint. His paintings decorated their house like windows into special moments of their shared past, views of rivers, villages, sea sides, mountains and lakefronts. Years afterwards, when he was no longer alive, speaking of those pictures, my grandmother said, "Well, of course to me they are all holidays!"

My recollection today is of those paintings, each unique, the traces lovingly left behind of shared travels — and of the framed black and white photo of my grandfather, sitting on his stool, wearing his brown felt hat, a brush in hand and another held in waiting between his teeth, ready for the next stroke, captured in time on his own creative journey.

Apparently spending money on experiences is more likely to bring us lasting happiness than spending money on objects. In the long run, we value our experiences more highly than ownership. While experience can live on in memory, material objects can fade and disappear from view.

Even missing the plane, losing our luggage or finding we have been double-booked when we finally arrive exhausted, can bring a smile years later when we share the stories. Connection with others through storytelling far exceeds the pleasure of acquiring material goods.

If the "story value" of memories outweighs the value of a material possession, perhaps it is a consideration when we are looking for those mementoes of a holiday. Maybe it is the souvenirs which have a personal story to tell which will gather additional meaning for us and not those picture-book, mass-produced, memorabilia sold in the tourist-trapping souvenir shops.

The Pursuit of Happiness

Our experiences are more important to us than our material purchases, says Thomas Gilovich in a paper entitled "A wonderful life: experiential consumption and the pursuit of happiness," which is the result of a twenty-year study:

You can really like your material stuff. You can even think that part of your identity is connected to those things, but nonetheless they remain separate from you. In contrast, your experiences really are part of you. We are the sum total of our experiences.

Experiences live on in the memories we cherish, the stories we tell, and the enhanced sense of self they help us construct.

What is more, in the study, the difference in people's downstream satisfaction with their experiential purchases was increased by how often they talked about them.

MAKING TANGIBLE THE INTANGIBLE…

Many of us will look for a holiday souvenir or memento. "I want to capture the experience of that time and place and hold on to it for a bit longer." Telling and retelling the stories of what we have seen and experienced is a way to hold dear the memories of that time in that place.

Souvenirs act as aide-mémoires, gifts, conversation pieces and evidence of our travels. Their physical presence helps to make tangible or to freeze in time a fleeting, transitory experience. We want to bring the extra, out-of-our ordinary back home with us, into our familiar and ordinary lives, as a reminder of that holiday magic.

According to the travel website Icelolly.com, the most popular souvenirs are ornaments, T-shirts, postcards, shot glasses, tattoos, sand in bottles, fridge magnets and tea towels. There is a scene in the film *If It's Tuesday, This Must Be Belgium* where the tourist who has been collecting "souvenirs" from every hotel the tour has stayed at, from embossed towels to logo-inscribed ashtrays, lifts his suitcase onto the coach. It opens up, much to his embarrassment, spilling all the contents…

Temple of Poseidon
Sounion, Greece

PARIS
FRANCE

GRECE GREECE

GREECE

Paris

From Transitory to Tangible

I thought of keeping a journal with an account of all our doings — and "just beings," trying to give you the holiday feeling by proxy since you are not here. But the days have passed as days do and I will save you some carefully selected shells instead of the whole beach. I think we have been apprentices in the art of not doing anything. It's not the same as doing nothing. It is like the difference between practising thinking of nothing or not thinking. One requires action, the effort of avoidance, and the other non-action, a letting go without resistance. So we have swum, we have dived, we have read and we have slept. We have eaten BBQs by night and picnics on the rocks by day. And the days and nights have flowed into each other so that we could forget the time, the dates, the beginning or the end. It is like floating on the waves here — you relax and let them carry you.

We live these days in parallel universes — diving under the water, feeling a part of that blue/green world with shoals of brightly-coloured fish our silent companions, and immersing ourselves in imaginary kingdoms through the pages of the books we read. Between the two we come up for air and refreshment which has never tasted so good.

So the seashells I bring you are like these words I send you, reminders of the salty tang of the sea, the touch of gentle breezes through the pines, the silence at sunset and the sight of the narrow shadow of the parasol as it casts its line of shade where I sit now, writing to you from the beach.

How can we hold on to these times that seem to pass so fast, or prolong the pleasures and bring back the treasures we uncover on holiday? Can we share our delight with others, or offer them a sprinkling of the holiday magic that we have encountered?

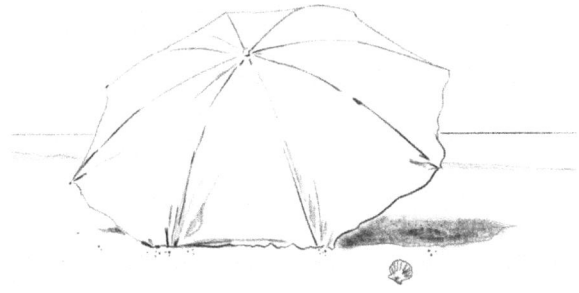

From Tangible to Transitory

Several years ago, our youngest son brought back soursop seeds from Hawaii, contrary to the Canadian Food Inspection Agency's regulations. The seeds, once dried then soaked, sprouted for a short time and looked as though they might even grow so many miles away from home, but then succumbed to homesickness, to the lack of sunshine, the absence of the scent of tropical flowers, the soft trade winds and the sound of the South Pacific rolling in on sandy beaches...

For a short time around April, the cherry blossoms in Vancouver are magnificent. In Japan, cherry blossoms are prized for the very impermanence of their beauty. There, families take time off to enjoy the short-lived blossom season, picnicking under the trees. However, spring-time visitors to Stanley Park can be seen cutting off blossom-laden branches to take home where they are unlikely to last any longer than they would on the tree. While they could continue to be enjoyed for a little more time in the park by the many instead of the few who so desperately want to capture their beauty, there is no-one who can change their transitory nature. The treasure of those magical blossom days will be held within by all who witness their delicacy and experience the fleeting nature of their beauty.

Mono No Aware

In the Japanese Buddhist tradition, there is an expression to describe the appreciation of things in the shadow of their future absence: *Mono No Aware* is a concept born in the Heian period (794–1185), a time of great cultural flourishing. It describes a fleeting, fragile beauty that cannot be pinned down to a single moment or image. It leaves nothing behind but a memory or hint of what might have been there. This fragility actually strengthens the power of its beauty:

The beauty lies not in [the] object itself, but in the whole experience, transformation, and span of time in which the object is present and changing...

The emotion associated with the object changes as the situation varies. Thus, one must constantly adapt to the changing feeling in the object, which ultimately heightens the participant's sensitivity for finding the beauty in *mono no aware*. One may feel a sense of joy at the sight of a beautiful, full blossom of *sakura* [cherry blossom]. In a few hours or days, however, that blossom may have already wilted or fallen to the ground. The observer must remember each component of this process.

FROM TRANSITORY TO LASTING

Like filling a time capsule addressed to our future selves or a photo of a single moment frozen in the pages of an album, acquiring a souvenir is a deliberate attempt to capture the intangible and the transitory for later enjoyment. The perfect souvenir can arrive in as many forms as the travellers who collect them — the functional one that you use regularly for years to come, the sentimental kind that makes you smile every time you see it, and the truly unique one that starts a conversation, invites you to tell its story.

But, even the most tangible souvenir has a shelf life of meaning equivalent to the time we are here to tell its tale. Gathering dust or confined to a cupboard, it is easy to forget on which of your grandmother's trips to Holland she acquired those little windmill salt and pepper shaker twins or whether in fact they came from somebody or somewhere else. As time passes, stories change, and what once carried one person's memories may sit unnoticed or neglected — or begin a new life carrying the associations attached by a new owner.

Souvenirs

Our children each had the opportunity to choose something meaningful to them by which to recall their many happy holiday visits with grandparents from before the time they could first remember.

One son was captivated by a Mille Fiori glass paper weight. Tiny button-sized flowers nestle on a bed of soft tissue-like fabric all under a glass dome that alternately magnifies and shrinks the colourful contents. That there is a crack on one side and the bottom is chipped adds to the uniqueness of his grandfather's paperweight. For him, there is magic and mystery in the optical illusion that draws him into an inexplicable world where his grandfather continues forever to sit at his desk, poring over papers, looking up when his grandson enters the room. For my father, the association with his own mother and with her house made that paperweight special. I cannot picture that time or that place, nor do I know how she had acquired it. A different story at a different time imbues the same object with memories and meaning, like a dream catcher that absorbs and releases without allowing an accumulation of dreams to change its form.

Pan Con Tomate

One of my favourite souvenirs both inspires a memory of happy holidays and is a reminder to savour the present every time I revisit it.

When we spent family holidays in a house very close to the sea, we could jump off the rocks for a morning, afternoon or evening swim. As a pre-breakfast wake-up, nothing compared before or has equalled since that refreshing dip into the magical underwater world where sea grasses sway to invisible breezes and shoals of tiny fish move as one, gracefully, silently sweeping out of the path of oncoming human traffic. A quick shower to wash off the salt, then the purchase of today's fresh bread and some gloriously flavourful tomatoes. This is the recipe for *Pan Con Tomate* or *Pan Tumaca*, to be enjoyed with *café con leche* and an appetite that only the sea can bring.

INGREDIENTS:

- 8 slices of bread, toasted (pan rustico — if possible some sort of pan paysan)
- 1 garlic clove peeled and cut in half
- 3 or 4 tomatoes (Sa tomàtiga de ramallet are the traditional Mallorquin tomatoes with lots of flavour)

METHOD:

1. Rub the garlic clove on the toasted bread and add a drizzle of olive oil.
2. Rub the tomatoes over the toasted, oiled bread.
3. Sprinkle with a pinch of salt.

11

Mushin:
The Art of Vacating

*We must be willing to let go of the life
we have planned, so as to have the life
that is waiting for us.*

—JOSEPH CAMPBELL

*The real voyage of discovery
consists not in seeing new lands
but in seeing with new eyes.*

—MARCEL PROUST

In addition to filling our holidays with happy memories, we may consider the purpose of a vacation as a freedom or release from duty, business or activity. The word "vacation" is derived from the Latin word *vacare*, meaning to be empty, free or at leisure. While we often try to fill our holidays with fun activities, there is also the opportunity to empty ourselves of the obligations of everyday life and our preoccupation with whatever comes next. In the study mentioned in Chapter 2, from the *Applied Research in Quality of Life Journal*, the only vacationers who experienced an increase in happiness after their trip were those who reported feeling "very relaxed" while they were away. Even for this small group, the effect only lasted for two weeks before returning to baseline levels. How do we become "very relaxed" on holiday?

Letting Go

In earlier years when children were small, we spent family holidays in a villa with a swimming pool. When we went for this annual longed-for family vacation, we would reach our destination after a long drive from the north of Spain, the final leg of which was usually the overnight ferry from Barcelona. Arriving travel-worn and tired, each year he would initiate the holiday by jumping into the pool with clothes on. No matter for how many years this tradition continued, we never failed to be surprised and delighted to see him wash off the dust of the journey and the soot of the year in one spontaneous leap. It was as though he was saying "Let the show begin!" — and our holiday "performance" was the welcome intermission between the acts of a workaday world.

It is easy to suppose that we go on vacation to either get away from the humdrum or the stress of daily life or to experience, if only for a short time, the luxury of leisure and the enjoyment of activities we cannot pursue at home. Are we getting away from the feelings we associate with overwork or are we being drawn to our expectations about the rewards of holiday time? Or is it both? It is like the choice between sticks or carrots.

Sticks or Carrots?

When we ran our small hotel in the mountains of northern Spain most of our personnel came from the small villages in the area. Happy to have employment when there was little available, especially in the winter months, many of our staff were prepared to work anywhere they were needed — behind the scenes in the kitchen, serving the food themselves that they had prepared, cleaning the rooms, or answering the phone and making reservations. We found that very many were not used to the liberty, the responsibility, or the trust we placed in them, having been brought up with the "stick" and threatened by punishment if they did not conform. We on the other hand, northern Europeans, believed wholeheartedly in the "carrot" approach, offering rewards for taking on more responsibilities. Sometimes it backfired when someone seemed to take advantage of our generosity, assisted by the Spanish labour laws, although mostly we saw a growing sense of pride, belonging and loyalty — and the simple pleasure of doing a job well.

In between the relief of escape and the anticipation of reward, there are moments when we truly enjoy our vacation time, when we are neither thinking about what we are glad to have left behind nor planning the distractions we are hoping to experience on holiday. To relax is to loosen our grip on what came before or what will come next and to be here now. By being "empty, free or at leisure," we can better appreciate what we are doing in the moment. Being on vacation is an opportunity to let go of the past, to detach from concerns for the future and to live in the ever-unfolding, unpredictable present which becomes its own intrinsic reward. It can be a time to practice the art of doing nothing, even for a short time. It gives us a chance to notice what emerges from that space of no thought, no action, without rehearsal or plans, a spontaneous, improvised version of life.

A Butterfly in February

Many years ago, on the day my father died I recall sitting outside on the step, just in front of the door, protected from the winter wind and enjoying the weak February sunshine. An unseasonal butterfly appeared from somewhere, drawing me into the present moment. I watched in fascination as it too felt the warmth on its wings. It was the intermission in which to let go of a week filled with farewells before the next act, when all the many end-of-life formalities would begin. In that moment I felt gratitude for the richness and the relief of being fully present, a brief interlude, a "vacation" between the past and the future, a deep breath, a moment of respite while, with kindness, time stood still. It is the stillness I remember...

If only for a short time, while we allow ourselves to be on vacation, we have the chance to practise living in what some would call a meditative state by being attentive, present, mindful and aware.

You may ask then, what is the difference between a "meditative state" and the practice of meditation? While meditation is itself a "doing," a meditative state is "being." To achieve a meditative state, we may practice meditation or find another technique or goal-oriented activity such as being in the mountains or listening to music to uncover a place of stillness. If you believe that your feelings of peace come from meditating, from mountains or from music, you might think that you have to always go to that practice, that place or that music to recover the same peaceful feelings. Sometimes that works and sometimes it doesn't.

If you miss your meditation practice, you may judge yourself, then assume your stressed state of mind is the result of failing to practise. If the mountains or the music do not bring you the same endorphins, the same state of equanimity each time, it is easy to suppose that you have to keep going back to try to recapture that feeling or find another path to peace. If you cannot find your way, you may feel discouraged, disillusioned or in despair.

Where Is the Butterfly?

If later, I had returned to the doorstep to find that feeling of peacefulness, it would have been like hoping to see another rare February butterfly and instead finding disappointment. Becoming aware of and grateful for the experience of even a short interlude of stillness leads to further depths of peacefulness that emerge without search or practice.

If you consider the state of meditation your *natural* state, your default setting, you will realize that to find it requires an *emptying* of expectation and letting go of action rather than an addition of more activities and obligations. Then you may find that a meditative state comes more easily and more often, especially when you allow yourself to spend time in the intermission between acts, wherever you are and whatever you are doing.

If peace of mind is already present within you, then each of these practices are pathways connecting you with what is already there. While one day you may choose to meditate, another day you may hike in the mountains or listen to music, whatever calls to you on that day — and you awaken to what was there all along, inside you.

The Law of Resonance

When two tuning forks are mounted on sound boxes near each other, striking one will cause the other to vibrate. When one vibrates, the second will also vibrate because the energy carried by the sound wave through the air is *tuned* to the frequency of the second tuning fork. Since the incoming sound waves share the same natural frequency as the second tuning fork, that tuning fork also easily begins vibrating at its natural frequency.

If, as "receptors," our minds are cluttered with a lot of extraneous thoughts, it is hard to receive any signals from outside. When we are in a receptive state, we "tune in," but if it were not for an *innate* receptiveness, there could be no resonance. In that case, neither meditation, nor mountains nor music would touch us. As conscious "tuning forks," we can let go of distraction and be present for whatever shows up.

Holiday stress has been well documented — health problems, homesickness, relational problems or culture shock can all contribute to a less than carefree holiday. Vacations can be exhausting with travel delays and endless queues for holiday attractions. The demands and expectations for entertainment placed upon parents can lead to parental wear out.

A Different Way of Being

Truth, like gold, is to be obtained not by its growth,
but by washing away from it all that is not gold.
— Leo Tolstoy

When we arrived at a holiday home, despite clamours
for entertainment, whether beach picnics or night-time
trips to the town, we would explore the small library of
paperbacks usually left by the owners for the
enjoyment of their guests. Instead of being laden with
books to bring with us, we would delight in the opportunity to choose from a limited selection and to read
something new. Sometimes we would spend hours
absorbed in the kinds of books we would never have
considered picking up at home.

Rather like trying on the costume of a holiday
persona for the duration of a visit, our holidays
became an opportunity to consider a different way
of dressing, eating, reading — and being.

It was through these welcome, unsolicited
discoveries on one of our holidays that I came
across Paulo Coelho's books. *The Alchemist* touched
me, reawakening the quest to find my own
"treasure." Each year when we returned to that
same villa, I eagerly anticipated another of Coelho's
books on the shelf — and was never disappointed as
the owners must have appreciated his books as
much as I did. After a few days, with energy
restored and appetites for activity recovered, the
plan for a family adventure would emerge...

Out of silence and stillness arise new ideas, new adventures waiting to be discovered, but just as consciously making happy memories seemed like an impossibility, so it might appear that the idea of spontaneity by design is an oxymoron.

So often we treat time as though it is space, supposing that we can change the irreversible past or hold on to the constantly evolving present in order to create a future to our liking. Vacating is the basis for extemporization (literally outside time). To be in the flow of spontaneous creation, we need to let go, not to seek. All the arts recognize and utilize creation in the moment. With freedom from self-judgement, we are open to inspiration. Improvisation is a requirement for yoga practitioners, martial artists, painters, actors, singers, dancers, sculptors, poets, writers — and vacationers alike.

Mushin

Mushin is a Japanese term meaning a state of mind that is not fixed, nor cluttered by thoughts or emotion.

What is Mushin in Practice?

Zen Calligraphy:
To write with mastery, one must clear one's mind and let the letters flow, without the intensity of effort.

Karate and Other Martial Arts:
Mushin is achieved when the mind is free of rambling thoughts, anger, fear, and particularly, free of ego. When *mushin* is achieved during combat, there is an absence of loose or random thoughts. It leaves the karate practitioner free to act without hesitation. Instead, he reacts without conscious effort, according to the training that has gone before and brought him to this point.

When we release the obligations and routines that often seem to dictate our regular lives, we find time to taste the true meaning of *vacare*.

If it is possible to let go of the past, to detach from concerns for the future and to live in the present, in a state of surrender, we may find a new level of relaxation.

We have a choice, to strive to fill our every holiday moment with action-packed activity or to take some time to let go of the layers...

We can join Rudyard Kipling in his advice to

fill the unforgiving minute
With sixty seconds' worth of distance run

or stay still, finding "thin times," like "thin places" where the veil between the sacred or the timeless and what we see as every day, timed reality, is translucent:

And it's only by going nowhere—by sitting still or letting my mind relax—that I find that the thoughts that come to me unbidden are far fresher and more imaginative than the ones I consciously seek out.

—PICO IYER, *The Art of Stillness*

Perhaps, on vacation, there is time for both.

The *Camino de Santiago*

The Camino de Santiago, mentioned in Chapter 9, is the most important pilgrimage route of all Europe. It has been travelled for centuries by millions of people to visit the tomb of Saint James the Apostle in Santiago de Compostela in northern Spain. Enjoying contact with nature, escaping from routine and disconnecting from the big cities are only some of the attractions. There are other benefits:

At the end of the road, when you arrive in Santiago, you will understand that your path has not ended, but is about to begin. As Paulo Coelho, author of *The Pilgrimage*, writes:

> The stone church is the same as it has been for centuries, but by the journey's end, it is the pilgrim who has been indelibly changed. Along the way, each traveller discovers how little he really needs to get along in life. After three days' walking, everyone ends up shedding half the weight in his backpack. Lighten the load, preserve the body, and tend the soul. Those are the lessons of Santiago de Compostela, the city at the end of the road best taken on foot, as it has been for centuries, one step at a time.
>
> **—PAULO COELHO**

12

Saudade:
Sweet Sorrow

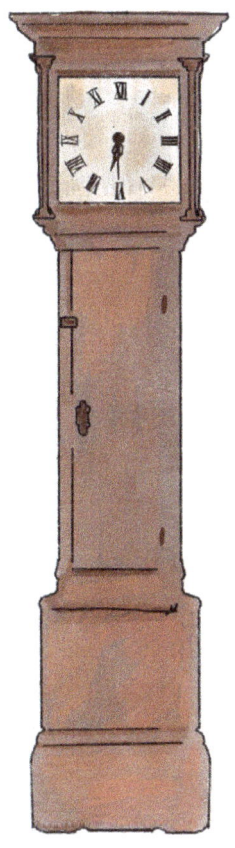

I've come to the end of my trip... One that I've been so fortunate to have, but one that I made happen — I challenged myself to travel alone for the first time in my life, a life in which I've seen depths and loss which have left scars, scars that have spurred me on to find new meaning... Forced myself to make my own decisions on everything, trust my instincts... I've thrown my arms open to the universe and said "lead me where you will"... And it has been so good to me, I have been so spoiled, it has truly shocked me...

I've cried, laughed, loved and lived every minute as if it were my first on earth, beaming inanely whilst walking, cycling, deeply listened and made connections with friends, old and new, and acquaintances at bars, in hotels, on the streets...

And I'm excited to be heading home as me, having shed layers of insecure thinking and false beliefs about myself I've gathered throughout my life, seeing for the first time that I am enough.

—DAVE YOUNG, Facebook post, February 2020

M any of us experience reluctance to leave a holiday destination — especially one we have enjoyed. The last days before returning home can sometimes be marred by the thought of our approaching departure. We are reminded once again that we are in that place, but not of that place. Rebecca Solnit describes the phenomenon in *A Field Guide to Getting Lost*, "The far became the near and the near far." Now it is time to reverse the orientation again, to leave "the far" and return again to "the near" of home. Thoughts of returning to work or school can hang heavy about us. The time we have been away seems to have flown by all too quickly, and yet when we recall our arrival at our holiday destination, it can also feel like a long time ago, something referred to as "The Holiday Paradox," the clash between the self experiencing time and the self remembering time.

We shall not cease from exploration
And the end of all our exploring
Will be to arrive where we started
And know the place for the first time.

—T.S. ELIOT, Little Gidding

Time Warps

Memories and markers in time are two key elements of the way we experience time. Holidays provide the perfect conditions for time to pass quickly — disruption to a daily routine and the removal of cues to the hours passing, combined with a host of new sights and sounds to absorb the attention. The days appear to fly by. ... The reason you feel as though you've been away for ages is that so many new things have happened that you have far more memories than in a normal week, warping your standard mental measurement of time.... The Holiday Paradox is caused by the fact that we view time in our minds in two very different ways— prospectively and retrospectively. Usually these two perspectives match up, but it is in all the circumstances where we remark on the strangeness of time that they don't.

—CLAUDIA HAMMOND, *Time Warped*

Whether the time away seems short or long, the thought of re-entering the familiar can be accompanied by a pre-nostalgia, a nostalgia that can easily dampen those last few days. It is easy to let the imminence of our departure bring a heaviness which can override our delight in today. How tempting it is to wish we could turn the clock back...

Father Time Stops the Clock

For many years whilst living in Canada, my parents celebrated New Year's Eve with a party, inviting friends, neighbours and family at home for the holidays, for an evening of fun — guessing games, a treasure hunt, charades and of course an elaborate dinner, all prepared days beforehand by my mother. Guests would arrive, often trudging through the snow, to the front door. Warm and inviting, the House-By-The-Water welcomed everyone who passed its stone threshold and had done so for more than two centuries.

There would be music performed by guests — violin, cello, piano and once or twice "The Toy Symphony," including a cuckoo water whistle, a rattle, triangles, makeshift drums and a xylophone. My father always accompanied everyone on the piano, a piano that had been built in the year he was born and had travelled with us across the Atlantic and has traversed it twice since.

That last night of the old year was always the longest of the entire twelve months, not least because my father would stop the stately grandfather clock that had kept time faithfully for nearly two hundred years when midnight got too close. While the clock stood patiently by, we were able to continue our festivities until it was more convenient to toast the arrival of the New Year. Only then, when the pendulum started to swing again, did we raise our glasses to welcome the next year as the clock loyally struck twelve at whatever the hour. For those minutes of reprieve, time stood still while we continued to celebrate its passing.

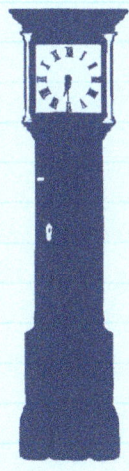

This Too Shall Pass...

Although the adage, "this too shall pass" is ascribed to the work of medieval Persian Sufi poets, the story also appears in Jewish folklore:

> King Solomon once searched for a cure against depression. He assembled his wise men together. They meditated for a long time and gave him the following advice: Make yourself a ring and have thereon engraved the words "This too will pass." The King carried out the advice. He had the ring made and wore it constantly. Every time he felt sad and depressed, he looked at the ring, whereon his mood would change and he would feel cheerful.
>
> **—Israel Folklore Archive # 126**

Yet, as Abraham Lincoln pointed out in an address in 1859 in which he recounts a similar tale about "an Eastern monarch," the reminder that nothing is permanent is as appropriate in times of peace and contentment as it is in times of trouble and discontent:

> How chastening in the hour of pride! How consoling in the depths of affliction!
>
> **—An address by ABRAHAM LINCOLN before the Wisconsin State Agricultural Society, September 30, 1859**

The awareness that "this too shall pass" can be both sweet and bitter. Transience brings its own beauty, perhaps best described in English by Juliet speaking to Romeo in Shakespeare's play:

Parting is such sweet sorrow that I shall say goodnight till it be morrow.

—WILLIAM SHAKESPEARE, *Romeo and Juliet*

Saudade is a Portuguese word that describes a yearning for something past, both the sadness from knowing that it is over and the happiness you feel as you recall the experience. Experiencing *saudade* is in fact a sign of how good something has been:

Saudade is a delicious cocktail of sadness and love, a tonic for a heart that longs to feel what it means to be human.

—CELINE DA COSTA, "Words Beyond Translation: Saudade"

Fairy Dust

We were to have left on Christmas Day to return to Spain in time for preparations for the New Year's Eve five-course dinner and dancing celebration that took place every year for a full house of guests at the hotel. While others feasted and celebrated the *Nochevieja* and the *Año Nuevo*, we were at our busiest. For us the days of fiestas were working Holy Days.

It had been a special holiday visit for us, a family celebration of the Winter Solstice and, as we all knew, the last time we would see my mother. So it was with a strange thankfulness that we heard the news that the ferry on which we were to make the overnight return crossing from Portsmouth to Bilbao would not be running. The ship had collided with the dock in stormy weather and although no-one was hurt, it would be out of service until the hull could be repaired.

The alternative route via France gave us an extra 48 hours before we needed to leave. With our packing done and our good-byes already said we had the luxury of an unexpected respite.

During those two precious days, time stood quietly aside for us while we no longer regretted its passage, no longer anticipated my mother's passing, but savoured the extra hours together like the gift they were. Knowing that the end was in sight while still being fully present, celebrating life rather than already mourning its completion, I recall feeling as though some magical fairy dust had been sprinkled on each one of us so that we could remain enchanted within this unpredicted pause.

In *A Field Guide to Getting Lost,* Rebecca Solnit speaks about the "voluptuous pleasure" of sadness.

And when everything else is gone, you can still be rich in loss.

So, we are further challenged to live in the present without thought of what comes next, to live each hour, savouring each minute.

Much like feeling the first chill in the air after a summer of sunshine, we become more aware that these Holy Days too are passing but, like the cherry blossom, their beauty and their value are enhanced and not diminished by their transitory nature. The days before departure have their own charm, like the fall before winter, when colours are more vivid, sunshine more precious and the harvest ready to be brought within. The return home, like the oncoming change of season, holds promise for different delights and unanticipated pleasures.

Sunrise

On a last morning of a holiday filled with warmth and happy memories, I arose early for a yoga practice in a silent, sleeping household. Sun salutations towards the glorious globe rising, as it always rises there, as if from out of the depths of the sea.

Golden days in the water and on the sand, the scent of hot pines, the indigo and turquoise of little *calas*, watching the evening seagulls wending their way in groups back to a nightly resting place, all this and so, so much more. The *sardinas asadas*, the *patatas bravas* on the terrace by the little harbour, the *erizos de mar*, plucked with care from the depths, the laughter, the delight in the freedom of being in each moment of every day as it came to pass... The feeling of appreciation expressed in that morning greeting to the sun as it emerged with fiery majesty, is one with the memories I hold dear.

Before the last suitcase was closed, before the drive to the airport, I was there with the sun as it made its first appearance of almighty brilliance that day, giving thanks for the time we had spent, sealing the jars of holiday memories with gratitude for all that had come before.

13

Sehnsucht:
Longing for Time Past

The whole object of travel is not to set foot on foreign land; it is at last to set foot on one's own country as a foreign land.

—G. K. CHESTERTON

We step back into our former roles often with a sense of culture shock. We inherit our past selves like an heir to the estate of a deceased person who has to pick up the threads, for we are not ourselves. We are a new person who has gone through re-creation and, if we do not feel renewed the whole point of tourism has been missed.

—NELSON H. H. GRABURN

Somehow, the release from our familiar life has instilled a reflective quality in us that was not present prior to our travel experience. We recognize our former selves like the shadow of who we once were before we left. A feeling of renewal may not come immediately. Jetlag and laundry may bring us back to a more mundane reality, but with gratitude for the welcome feelings of comfort at being home again and the life we have chosen, we may become aware of greater ease and appreciation — for both the holiday and our safe return.

The Holiday Effect

It is always hard to see the purpose in wilderness wanderings until after they are over.
—John Bunyan, *The Pilgrim's Progress*

I have noticed that sometimes when I come back from a holiday, despite my initial reluctance to return, if I am patient with myself, those feelings of replenishment come to me unbidden. The less I try to find them, the more quickly I feel refilled. In fact, it is the awareness of the difference in myself that first lets me glimpse the benefits. It is then that I begin to appreciate the change. Shifts in self-awareness lead to a deeper understanding and feeling grateful for them prolongs the holiday effect. By being in familiar surroundings once again I notice the difference in myself and experience the subtle changes more consciously.

The magic that allowed us to find pleasure in small things when we arrived at our holiday destination stays with us as we encounter once more the familiar of home with "fresh eyes."

> *I cannot see that door. I cannot see that chair:*
> *because a cloud of sleep and custom has come*
> *across my eyes. The only way to get back to them*
> *is to go somewhere else; and that is the real object*
> *of travel and the real pleasure of holidays.*
> **—G.K. CHESTERTON, "The Riddle of the Ivy"**

For the very first moments, hours or days after returning home, we can see the details, take in each sight and sound as if for the first time. While not yet invisible and inaudible in their familiarity, before the new once more becomes the normal, we can appreciate the details of home.

> *It occurs to me that the secret of being fully here,*
> *walking in the skin of this planet, is to learn to*
> *see things as though I were looking at them for*
> *the first time, or the last. Nothing is too small*
> *then, too mundane, too unusual. Everything is*
> *wonder. Everything is magical. Everything moves*
> *my spirit...*
> **—RICHARD WAGAMESE, *Embers***

It is said that the best way to "recharge your batteries" is by "unplugging" yourself. It sounds contradictory if the power source is outside. However, when the batteries are *self*-charging, with an internal power supply, all it takes is some time left alone to do their job.

It's the perspective we choose—not the places we visit—that ultimately tells us where we stand. Every time I take a trip, the experience acquires meaning and grows deeper only after I get home and, sitting still, begin to convert the sights I've seen into lasting insights.

—**PICO IYER,** *The Art of Stillness*

The Reset Button

Shortly after returning from holiday several years ago, I attended a meeting with several colleagues. One of my companions asked, "What is different about you?" Newly bronzed arms and sun-lightened hair did not seem to me to offer proof of a holiday since it was summertime both at home and where I had travelled. I wondered what that difference she noticed might be. It was not the colour of my skin or hair.

A break from routine, a release of customary pressures is like pushing the reset button, starting afresh on a new page whilst having a glimpse of the possibilities of a whole book spread out before you. There is a calmness that accompanies your return to the familiar when you have expanded your horizons. This new perspective on the small world we each inhabit brings more understanding, more patience, greater curiosity and an openness to looking at a bigger picture.

Perhaps my colleague sensed my detachment from the details of our customary connection.

Part of our homecoming experience is likely the bitter sweetness of nostalgia, *saudade*, a reminder of transience.

There can also be the "longing" you feel when you return from travelling and wish you could begin all over again with even more enjoyment, more delight and no stalling hesitation to dive in from high up on the rocks or squeamish reluctance to try that local dish. *Sehnsucht*, a German word for yearning, also includes those "life longings" for completion and perfection when experiences feel unfinished and imperfect and you crave the chance to repeat them. C.S. Lewis, of Narnia fame, describes the feeling as

> *an unsatisfied desire which is itself more desirable than any other satisfaction. I call it Joy ... anyone who has experienced it will want it again.*
>
> —C.S. LEWIS, *Surprised by Joy*

Both *saudade* and *Sehnsucht*, for which there are no one-word translations into English, express a little differently the nostalgia for a time that has passed. We recognize that what was so eagerly anticipated has now come and gone. Whether we wish we could have done it differently or we just feel sadness that the holiday is over, a reminder of impermanence is always bittersweet, the "particular kind of unhappiness or grief" which is "a kind we want." As Rebecca Solnit writes in *A Field Guide to Getting Lost*,

> *We treat desire as a problem to be solved, address what desire is for and focus on that something and how to acquire it rather than on the nature and the sensation of desire, though often it is the distance between us and the object*

of desire that fills the space in between with the
blue of longing. I wonder sometimes whether with
a slight adjustment of perspective it could be
cherished as a sensation on its own terms...If you
can look across the distance without wanting to
close it up, if you can own your longing

An awareness of the ephemeral nature of beauty and of life can bring greater appreciation for those memories. Families in Japan stop to enjoy all stages of the cherry blossom because seeing the fragile beauty in impermanence is its own reward. In Brazil, the 30th of January is the *Dia de Saudade,* a day to remember people who have gone and feel gratitude for times that have passed, a day to celebrate the bittersweetness of transience.

For some, the return from holiday brings a desire to finally make the change you have thought of making but had not previously found the courage to initiate.

As Vietnamese monk, Thich Nhat Hanh reminds us,

The path around our home
Is also the ground of awakening

Losing Weight by Not Trying

A few years ago, one son and his family spent a month in Umbria for work and for pleasure. After a week, he let go of his daily workout regime, left his vegetarian diet behind and permitted himself pizza and Peroni, or pasta and the local Montefalco Sagrantino. Most of all, he says, he stopped avoiding and began enjoying and very soon found himself in a new rhythm — a Martini Bianco, an evening walk around the Roman fortress at the top of the hill and a willingness to surrender the stressful thinking he had brought with him. When they returned from Italy, he was surprised and delighted to discover that he had lost ten pounds — by *not* trying.

The greater gift was his awareness that it was a release of pressures and the enjoyment of the pleasure of eating, not the suppression of appetite that had brought about the weight loss.

"Post-vacation blues" may be an expression of a dissatisfaction you have with where and how you are living. Rather than mourning the end of a holiday, you have realized, without having to receive notice on your tenancy or to break a leg, that it is time to move on or to change your lifestyle. Break-ups and other big life decisions can be as much a follow-on to a two-week vacation as the result of months of arduous deliberation at other times. Having seen something out-of-your-ordinary, you are no longer content with the familiar and feel confident to explore a new path.

Sometimes holidays are life-changing, from meeting a stranger with whom you will share your life, to deciding to move across a country, to changing careers, deciding to follow your dreams or realizing that the life you had left behind is no longer the one you choose to return to. All because of a few short weeks away from the day-to-day reality to which you were accustomed.

And for those of us ready to reacclimatize, with a little forethought on how we re-enter the world of work, school or home and our familiar routines, we can extend the post-vacation happiness quotient.

Post-vacation Blues (PVB)

A person may suffer from post-vacation blues after returning home or to a normal routine from a long vacation, especially if it was a pleasurable one. The longer a trip lasts, the more intense the post-vacation blues may be. This is because after the person returns home, they may believe their normal lifestyle routine is boring and unsatisfactory when compared to the activities they did while on their holiday/vacation. It is easier to overcome/adjust to a normal routine the shorter the trip was. Post-vacation blues may result in tiredness, loss of appetite, strong feelings of nostalgia, and in some cases, depression. Jetlag may intensify the post-vacation blues.

—WIKIPEDIA

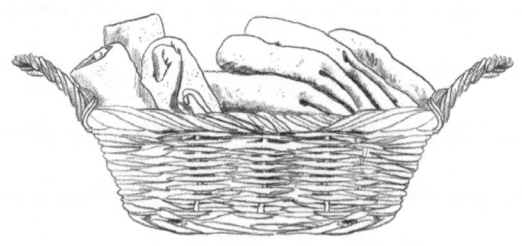

Jars of joyful memories may line the storage shelves of our minds. Those jars that were less sweet may be best left unopened, reminding us of the recipes that did not turn out so well, left to gather dust at the back, until we can bring the sweetness of laughter to improve their flavour.

Postcards, photos, mental snapshots of the highlights, there to decorate and remind, little aide-mémoires that conjure up again the magic of a moment, are worth savouring. Putting a memento of your trip on your desk, changing your screen saver to show your favourite vacation photo are simple visual cues that are an easy yet powerful reminder to relive how you felt on vacation. Now, any time you find work getting stressful, you can take a breath and go back to the peaceful feelings you felt while you were away.

Once the holidays are over, you can keep the holiday spark alive in your heart. Treating yourself well by limiting work commitments, leaving work on time and resisting the urge to check the backlog of emails on the first day, can ease you into a healthier work ethic than the one you left. Continuing to eat better, spending more time outside unplugged or exercising more frequently can be holiday habits worth holding onto.

In addition to having the cupboard stocked with some post-holiday delights, left there by your thoughtful pre-holiday self, or appreciating those in-between days you perhaps arranged, planning some fun things to do in those first weeks back can help to prolong your holiday spirit. Among the plans may be those for your next vacation...

Plan Your Vacation

The last Tuesday in January is "Plan Your Vacation Day," a national holiday in the United States initiated in 2018 by the US Travel Association in order to address the great number of unused vacation days. In addition to stimulating domestic tourism, the goal was for Americans to:

> enjoy stronger bonds with their families, greater fulfillment in their work lives, and enhanced health and wellness as a result of time away from the office
>
> —**GARY OSTER,** *Project: Time Off*

Many people however don't take time away from work because they think that their manager's perception of them will suffer as a result.

Shawn Ancor, a positive psychologist and author shows that the opposite is true. He is employed by the US Travel Association to promote the business case for taking time off. In an article written for the Harvard Business Review, he gives reasons why taking a vacation increases your chances of getting a raise or promotion.

In fact, he tells us, those who take all their vacation time have a 6.5% higher chance of getting a promotion or a raise than people who leave eleven or more days of paid time off unused.

A "positive and engaged brain" is "the greatest competitive advantage in the modern economy." In his book *The Happiness Advantage*, Shawn describes research which shows that when the brain is thinking positively, productivity increases by 31%, sales grow by 37%, and creativity and revenues can triple.

To be fully engaged at work, your brain needs regular

breaks. A change in perspective also replenishes your energy.

According to research conducted by the US Travel Association, when managers were asked what vacation time benefit would motivate them to encourage their employees to use more vacation days, they reported the top benefit was increased personal happiness (31%) followed by productivity (21%). Most managers realize that happy employees are also more inclined to be collaborative.

As Shawn also points out, you are taking a "voluntary pay cut" when you work instead of going on vacation if paid vacation is included among your employment benefits:

Four out of ten employees say that they can't take their vacation because they have too much work to do. But, think about it this way: whether or not you take a vacation, you're still going to have a lot of work to do. Life is finite, and work is infinite.

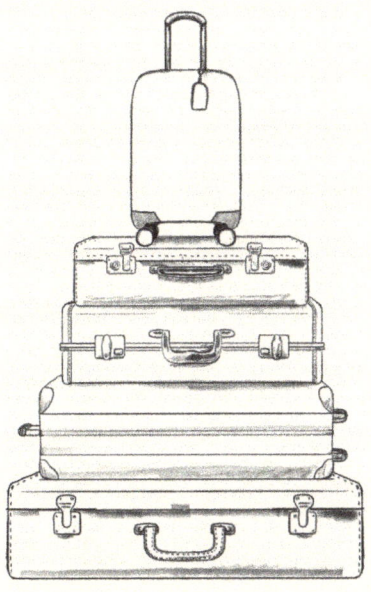

Holy Day Inns

So where do we go next?

It may sound like the relentless cry of a spoilt child at Christmas time — "What else?" "Is there another one for me?" Perhaps it is not really a demand for more gifts but the longing for more of the excitement of unwrapping. Who would not choose a continuation of this feeling of carefreeness, this spirit of adventure, this experience of living in the moment? Who wouldn't want to carry on exploring, greeting each new day as a first in the unforeseeable future? No limits, no end — on the road again.

As a way of being we can remind ourselves that there is always somewhere else to go. If it helps to plan the next getaway when you have just returned from holiday, why not? As Pooh Bear is reputed to have said, "Sometimes the anticipation is better than the honey."

Depending on time off and the perennial question of the pocketbook, you may or may not be able to book the time or space. It may be sufficient to dream and to browse, to talk "holidays" with friends. Exchanging vacation stories can take you there without airport queues, lost luggage or jetlag.

Those who love Christmas and all that it brings, the festivities, the family gatherings, the generosity and the time to enjoy being with loved ones, may find ways to begin celebrating early and to prolong the Christmas glow. Decorations sometimes stay up until Easter when outside the world is still dreary and grey. There are Santa Claus parades in July and in some places "Christmas rooms," or entire Christmas shops where trees, lights and ornaments are available all year round, providing Christmas-hungry shoppers with the opportunity to bask in the warmth of Jingle Bells or rejoice with Rudolph to their heart's content.

Why not vacation rooms and stores to accompany Holiday Inns? Every holiday is as unique as the holidaymaker, but the excitement wouldn't be about the sights or the sand, the mountains or the museums, it would be about the wrap-around holiday feeling where time stands still, waiting for you to check-in and hop on board to savour every moment and to make happy memories.

14

Armchair Travel – A Pilgrim's Mindset

When friends ask me for suggestions about where to go on vacation, I'll sometimes ask if they want to try Nowhere, especially if they don't want to have to deal with visas and injections and long lines at the airport. One of the beauties of Nowhere is that you never know where you'll end up when you head in its direction, and though the horizon is unlimited, you may have very little sense of what you'll see along the way.

—PICO IYER

Travel is about attitude and aspiration as much as about geography. What is at stake is not discovering distant countries and exotic habits, but making the move out of ordinary space and time.

—LEONARD J. BIALLAS

In the time of the pandemic, it seemed that many of us had no choice but to go Nowhere. With the advent of lockdowns, quarantines, self-isolation and social distancing, this chapter on "Armchair Travel" may be more relevant than first appeared. Many people have either already experienced or will be continuing to practise the art of "staycationing".

Plans for the next vacation when circumstances permitted, dreams of travels far and wide provided momentary distractions, but what of the time we were obliged to spend at home?

Some, though reluctantly and perhaps involuntarily, had to learn how to travel, while staying still. Zoom, Skype and other plugged-in platforms for face-to-face conversation gave us at least the temporary illusion of mixing with people all over the world. Some of us suffered from Zoom fatigue, a virtual equivalent of jetlag. Others of us, not having signed up for the electronic experience, resisted the invitation to immerse ourselves in the world of technology and instant communication and found ourselves uncomfortably isolated in these times of unfamiliar off-line immobility.

Realizing that we are always en route and that as long as we live, we are already on a journey with no yet known destination is a first step in the art of being at peace with where we are now. As we get a little further on our way, we realize which direction we face and perhaps know that we are both on a quest for adventure and on our way home.

As we explore the possibilities of limited travel or staycationing, it may be helpful to recall some of the characteristics of a traveller's mindset which inspire vacating and becoming very relaxed.

LETTING GO OF THE FAMILIAR
LEADS TO SEEING WITH FRESH EYES

Exploration often depends on letting go of the familiar. Escapism or the perceived need for a break from daily life are concepts based on Western societies' ideas of leisure, a luxury afforded to the few. Yet tourism as we know it has grown from the idea of Holy Days, marked by a change from the usual routine, even for a day. Shabbat, the Jewish day of rest on the seventh day of the week, is a day of freedom from the regular labours of everyday life, an opportunity for reflection and for spending time with family. In Spain the origin of the countless fiestas lies in religious feasts, usually honouring a Saint's Day. Fortunately, for many of us it is often possible to release some of the obligations of daily life, if only for a short time, without leaving home. Changing schedules and the sequence and location of daily activities can give a fresh view of the familiar with a chance to explore an unknown that was under our noses but previously unseen.

There is wisdom in turning as often as possible from the familiar to the unfamiliar: it keeps the mind nimble, it kills prejudice, and it fosters humor.

—GEORGE SANTAYANA, *The Philosophy of Travel*

The Trolley

I recall when I was a child enjoying a morning breakfast on a grassy bank at home in the garden. To this day, many years later, I remember the taste of pineapple jam on toast under the trees. It must have been quite a job to bring everything outside on a sturdy wooden trolley, three children steadying the corners, or carrying cups, and a dog waiting to pick up anything that fell. The freshness of the morning, the smell of my parents' newly made coffee, the same colour as the brown Denby jug in which it steamed, made it all worth-while, and the memory still sits treasured in a jar on my shelf.

I can picture my parents, years later, with the same trolley, now painted a crisp, clean white with a blue and white patterned surface covering two shelves laden with supper things. I see glasses half-filled, and the decanter with homemade wine. Dark blue plates perched on their knees hold one of my mother's savoury vegetarian creations. "This is very good!", says my father, as he does for every meal she prepares, then the murmur of their quiet interchange fades...I see them sitting there together sometimes for an evening meal in a small cozy room, the library, the place we were called when my father wanted to have a "serious" conversation with any of us.

For those evenings it was their book-lined bistro, their night out from the usual, their in-house getaway while we, teenagers at the time, inhabited the kitchen.

LETTING GO OF EXPECTATIONS
LEADS TO BEING HERE NOW

Vacationing is a state of mind that can be accessed on holiday or staycationing at home. The unfamiliarity of being immobilized invites a journey inwards.

> *There is still a deep longing in our Western culture to wander towards wild places and to have this wayfaring lead to deep meaning, renewed ways of seeing, and back to our own sense of grounded belonging to this Earth and the communities in which we live.*
>
> **—THE SEATTLE SCHOOL, "Alumni Spotlight"**

It is as though we search in wild places to find ourselves again and to return to a feeling of belonging. With less opportunity to travel so far afield we may discover, like the shepherd boy, Santiago, in *The Alchemist*, that what we seek is already buried where we stand.

A picnic in your own garden can reveal a new world and a walk around the block can be an adventure when seen through fresh eyes.

> *The journey is into the undiscovered land of our own imagination, and the paths in our own backyards are the soil of awakening. Whatever we can find at a pilgrim shrine, we can find at home, for we are really reaching inward to the depths of our very being.*
>
> **—LEONARD BIALLAS,** *Pilgrim*

The camera lens through which we may have experienced new views as a tourist, becomes a fresh way of seeing magic in the minutiae, pattern in the prosaic and design in the dissonance. Instead of a barrier between us and the immediacy of our experience, it offers a view finder that helps us to uncover a world in a grain of sand.

Garden Reflections

Outside the window I see little yellow flowers, jostled and tousled by working bees, searching for sips of sweetness.

The other day I watched the bees as they ecstatically tumbled about in the pollen, like warm woolly puppies rolling in bliss. I had not noticed before their delight in the process of gathering nectar while simultaneously acting as unwitting, yet intended, pollinating agents. With their stripy fur dusted and wrapped like flour-coated morsels of pure joy, they seemed bent on their purpose, never doubting what they were there for or why or whether and when to look elsewhere for more...

It seems that we are the ones who question. Lost in thought we sometimes lose our way and forget that we too have purposes, both those we follow through our conscious intentions and the many additional blessings we can bestow, through the benefits of living our life in the pleasure of its process.

Who knows what pollination, what cross-fertilization is happening as we roll, rapturous in the powdered magic dust of creation?

Many years ago, on a blue and red squared blanket spread out on the grass in the garden, prey to exploring ants who were unaware of any border that separated us, I lay beneath a hot summer sun and read the beautiful short story by Virginia Woolf "Kew Gardens." Ever since, I have found myself entranced, seeing flower beds from the perspective of the creatures that look up from under the leaves through the dappled sunlight at the two-legged passers-by... seeing colourful blankets spread on green lawns as invitations to explore for those whose tiny, grass-forested worlds are sometimes invaded by tartan intruders...

An ordinary landscape seen through fresh eyes can offer possibilities for new experience and new adventure previously hidden from view.

EXPANDING OUR HORIZONS IS POSSIBLE IN TIME OR PLACE

When you have all the time in the world, you can spend it, not on going somewhere, but on being where you are.

—ROBIN WALL KIMMERER, *Braiding Sweetgrass*

Recalling the experience of teens who are able to substitute time travel for place travel, we may find that limitations on place travel present opportunities for noticing the breadth of other horizons close to home. In a wonderful chapter, "Witness to the Rain," Robin Wall Kimmerer writes about rainfall and time. Comparing the differences between raindrops, how they fall, where they fall, she reflects on the different experiences of time, depending on our viewpoint:

How can minutes and years, devices of our own creation, mean the same thing to gnats and to cedars?

Maybe there is no such thing as rain; there are only raindrops, each with its own story.... Maybe there is no such thing as time; there are only moments, each with its own story.

With our tendency for "thinking too much and listening too little," we can miss what is within our reach from where we stand. By opening our eyes and ears we can uncover a new world right here.

Around the Block

In *A Walk Around the Block: Stoplight Secrets, Mischievous Squirrels, Manhole Mysteries & Other Stuff You See Every Day (And Know Nothing About)*, journalist Spike Carlsen sets off to investigate everything he can about all the things we take for granted — from manhole covers and recycling bins to bike lanes and stoplights, to the antics of pigeons and the mischief of squirrels. Even the mundane can bring a sense of wonder when we walk with a different viewpoint.

Alexandra Horowitz, professor of psychology and expert in canine cognition, also takes readers around the block in *Eleven Walks with Expert Eyes*:

> To a surprising extent, time spent going to and fro ... is unremembered. It is forgotten not because nothing of interest happens. It is forgotten because we failed to pay attention to the journey to begin with ... I was paying so little attention to most of what was right before us that I had become a sleepwalker on the sidewalk.
>
> **—ALEXANDRA HOROWITZ, *On Looking***

Planes May Not Be Flying, but We Are...

Confined to home during the first outbreak of the pandemic, and unable to travel further than the return journey to the kitchen or the bedroom from the living room, one family created adventures that some might dream about. Both parents usually work away from home and their two children are dropped off, picked up from school or daycare with violin, tennis and English lessons week in and week out, spending less time together as a family than they would wish for. During the lockdown they were home together — or were they? For in their collective imaginations, they travelled near and far, from punting on the canals in Venice to time travelling to Ancient Rome and visits to modern day New York — all without leaving a carbon footprint, experiencing jet lag or needing to show a single passport. Sheets make good togas and a toy rubber dinghy provided a punt that grew large enough to transport the whole family.

Many years from now when the children look back on these fantastical voyages, will they have left a mark on their consciousnesses? Learning as learning should be — by doing, by being a part of an engaging experience and sharing the fun with those closest to you, isn't this the recipe for the best kind of learning, learning with the heart? Even the little one, only two and a half, will recall a time of feeling the warmth of family. He may not remember the details of the days spent in the company of both parents, the connection with a sister five years his senior, but the indelible mark of delight will remain...

Home Travel

During the pandemic, virtual tours were available for those looking for a taste of travel. Viator, a provider of tours and shore excursions worldwide, offered users a variety of virtual tours they called #RoamFromHome. These included sightseeing cities and global landmarks, art and history museums, safaris — even culinary excursions, and more. The options were expansive with a fee for select tours. Prices varied — a vegetarian cooking class in Tuscany was about US$38, while a Singapore-themed course was free. Some museum tours were complimentary, but a virtual Harry Potter–themed tour of London cost about US$5.

CELEBRATING THE TRANSIENT INVITES THE MAGIC OF GRATITUDE

We are often most aware of the "unforgiving minute" when we know that something is about to end. When we are not anticipating change we can easily bask in the apparent security of an endless present and perhaps take the details of our daily existence for granted. Celebrations such as the Japanese custom of picnics with family and friends under the cherry blossoms during *hanami* bring joy to what could otherwise be an uncomfortable realization of life's fleeting nature and an appreciation of the poignant beauty of transience.

Holidays and feast days, celebrations of life — and of death — can be opportunities to recognize and even rejoice in the impermanence of life. When we do something out-of-our-ordinary, we are more likely to acknowledge that we pass this way only once. If we can let go of the weight of this awareness of our mortality, we may find a new freedom which allows us to feel more gratitude for the sights and sounds along our way. The brevity of a holiday can bring a reminder of this truth that often goes unnoticed at home. Celebrations of every sort are opportunities to enjoy the moment while accepting that "this too shall pass." Without needing to leave home we can feel gratitude for whatever occasion we choose to honour.

A Celebration Every Day

At the Days of The Year website, you can find a good reason for celebration every day of the year. Believing that every day is special, the creators of this website have gathered a collection of weird and wonderful holidays. They list and explain the public-spirited themes for each month and describe some of the bizarre and unusual events to celebrate as "moments and occasions from around the world that bring people together."

For each day they provide the holiday's history and suggestions for how to acknowledge it. Today for example, the 25th of October, they list no less than five special days, ranging from "World Pasta Day" to "Punk For A Day Day" to "Sourest Day." Although "Sourest Day" began forty-five years ago, named in honour of someone with the name Sauer, it is now, or so they say, an opportunity to celebrate all things sour, including sour attitudes! October is also "Pizza Month" and appropriately for this time of year, "Black Cat Awareness Month," supporting much-maligned black cats who are apparently adopted from animal shelters at a rate fifty percent lower than any other colour of cat.

If you don't find anything here to suit your celebratory mood, the website also gives you the chance to create your own special holiday.

Special Occasions

One of our sons, without knowing about "Sourest Day," delighted in celebrating his own "Special Occasions" with a glass of vinegar. Whether he felt like the sharp, mouth-puckering taste, wanted to acknowledge what he considered to be a special event, or simply wanted to throw a party, he would raise his glass whenever the moment inspired him and, with eager anticipation, declare a "Special Occasion." Perhaps he had watched our example. Weaving together the traditions of two countries in a third meant that there were many opportunities for creating a festive family tapestry of celebration.

Christmas was one such time. The *Vacaciones de Navidad*, a season of secretive giving in many parts of the world, stretched for weeks in our household. It started on Christmas Eve, traditionally a family celebration in Spain. We often spent the days of Christmas in the empty hotel, spreading ourselves out in our favourite guest rooms like Goldilocks in the house of the Three Bears. We took over the well-equipped kitchen, preparing our special Swedish feast for *Nochebuena* (Christmas Eve) to eat in the hotel's spacious dining room. When our special Christmas meal was over there would be a loud banging on the door, and an appropriately dressed figure would appear. It was the Jultomten, the Swedish Christmas gnome who, in true Swedish tradition, would ask, "Are there any good children?" and express his disappointment once more that the "man of the house" had left just at the moment when he, the Tomten, had arrived!" They never did meet, so the hide and seek tradition continued for years with our children later joining in the magic by taking the part of Tomten's helpers.

Representing the English-speaking side of the family, I became "Mother Christmas" on chimney duty and responsible for the surreptitious stuffing of stockings. She was not as shrouded in mystery as the Swedish gnome and was never witnessed on active duty, but nevertheless she was as much a part of our festive tradition as her Swedish counterpart. Christmas Day was a day of thanks-giving in our home, for the gifts exchanged and for the opportunity for everyone to share in the creation of a family tradition and the spirit of generosity.

Next on our list of Christmas festivities was *Nochevieja* or *Año Nuevo*, the celebration of the "old night" and the arrival of the New Year, an especially important occasion for Spanish families and one that we enjoyed in good company at the hotel. Guests, mostly from Madrid, would join us for a five-course feast. At midnight the chimes would be broadcast on television from the Puerta del Sol, the central square in Madrid, and apart from the solemn sound of the *campanadas de fin de año*, ringing out the old year, there would be silence as everyone in the dining room attempted to eat twelve white grapes before the last bell was struck, ensuring good luck and prosperity for the year to come. After *las doce uvas de la suerte* (the twelve grapes of luck), the *cava* (Spanish sparkling wine) would flow and whistles, trumpets, noisemakers of every description would fill the space between the stone walls, echoing outside amongst the ancient oaks and chestnut trees and beyond, to where the sheep huddled close in the cabañas in wintery oblivion and up to the windswept Sierra del Cuera above, seen only by sailors on the stormy Mar Cantabrico. The merriment would continue with dancing to all the traditional Spanish favourites until the not-so-small hours.

Planning the menu, buying in provisions, including the elaborate *bolsas de cotillón* (party bags), decorating the hotel and booking staff for those days was a lot of preparation, and on those special occasions, income only just balanced expenses. The profit however was in the shared spirit of celebration, fiesta for fiesta's sake.

El Día de Los Reyes, coinciding with the Swedish custom of dancing around the Christmas Tree before disrobing it of its decorations, concluded our Christmas season — not without relief that the festivities were over for another year!

El Día de Los Reyes

In many English-speaking households, the busy commercial season is over with the last sale of Boxing Day week and the start of the New Year, but in the countries that celebrate the coming of the Three Kings, festivities continue until Epiphany or Twelfth Night. Traditionally, all over Spain, a regal and splendid procession of Los Reyes Magos on the eve of El Día de Los Reyes, the sixth of January, is followed by an evening of excitement when children can finally open the gifts that have been secretly left for them by the three royal visitors when they were out of the house watching or participating in the magnificent march. For those children who have not been good, this can include a lump of coal, which has become a sweet and popular punishment made by burning sugar until it is black. *El Roscón de Los Reyes*, a decorated sweet bread, is served for *Reyes*, contains another mysterious surprise — a hidden crown or even the Baby Jesus for the lucky finder.

HOLY DAY MAKING

Some of us find annual festivities an unwelcome reminder of times past. Celebrations repeated year after year can be difficult for many who prefer not to feel the clutches of nostalgia and attempt to avoid both the sweet sadness of *Saudade* and the wistful regret of *Sehnsucht*.

For those who "hate good-byes" and dread endings, who would rather not recall even the pleasurable memories in case they find the poignancy overwhelming, is it possible to consider acknowledging the beauty of transience for its own sake — with tears and laughter? Celebrating change and completion, enjoying the memories we have acquired, wherever we are on the journey, can bring appreciation for what has passed.

Instead of mourning life's passage, we can focus on celebrating whether at home or away. It may seem like some convivial attempt to dull the pain of recognizing our impermanence, but instead of regret that this precious time will soon be over, or has already passed, acknowledgement of transience can inspire gratitude. There is no lack of respect for the dead in an Irish wake, no suggestion that a celebration of life in any way negates the poignancy of its passing.

So many changes in life come without warning, but sometimes we know beforehand that this will be a once-in-a-lifetime holiday or a one-time event, and we can consider ourselves fortunate to receive the invitation to celebrate ahead of time. Aware that a chapter is about to end and knowing that a new one will begin, we have the choice in how we close the pages. Birth and death, marriage and divorce, a change in health or situation can be opportunities to take stock and to walk consciously with gratitude into the future.

Memories of Solstice Celebrations in the Moonroom

It was our family Solstice celebration. Three children and spouses, accompanied by eight grandchildren, travelling from three countries, gathered to meet, to greet and to say good-bye. My mother descended the stairs for the last time in regal procession, transported in her armchair by a son, two sons-in-law and one grandson, accompanied on the piano by my father playing Mozart's *Andante Grazioso*. We sat at candlelit tables in the "Moonroom" as it later came to be called. There was a roast turkey and a whole salmon, cooked lovingly by the chefs of the family. My mother, vegetarian for the previous twenty-five years, tried both. There were Christmas crackers with colourful hats and corny jokes. There was laughter and merriment and gifts exchanged according to the ruling of the magician's hat out of which names had been picked some weeks earlier so that each member of the family would bring a gift for one other person. My mother delighted in the serendipity and the magic of it all. I don't remember if there was dessert though it may well have been an early Christmas pudding with rum butter sauce or ice-cream for the little ones.

Overhead, above us all, the full moon rose on the remains of our family feast, shining its white light in corners and on candles, crumbs and crumpled serviettes left behind from an occasion that we each remember to this day with joy and appreciation for the opportunity to celebrate.

Sadness and joy are part of life in the present as well as life that has passed. Treasured memories are built from both, like skins of an onion, layer upon layer, over and over again, both softening and strengthening as time goes by.

Armchair Travel can provide opportunities to take out those jars of memories lining the storage shelves of our minds. We can relive the joy of the happy memories and, by bringing the warmth of understanding to those jars left behind to gather dust, we can improve their flavour, perhaps finding the sweetness of laughter. By celebrating today with gratitude, we make Holy Days, turning memories into gold.

15

Duende: *The Alchemy of Home*

Home is within me and always was.

—RICHARD WAGAMESE

The words are no more than signposts. That to which they point is not to be found within the realm of thought, but a dimension within yourself that is deeper and infinitely vaster than thought. A vibrantly alive peace is one of the characteristics of that dimension, so whenever you feel inner peace arising as you read, the book is doing its work and fulfilling its function as your teacher; it is reminding you of who you are and pointing the way back home.

—ECKHART TOLLE

In both the insatiable hunger of the adventurer and the withdrawal experienced by the thwarted traveller, there is a desperate craving for more of the travel experience, like an inescapable addiction. Yet also implicitly, for the hungry and the restless, there is the apparently contradictory longing for a "way back" to satiation and stillness. Maya Angelou describes it as an "ache for home" that

> *lives in all of us, the safe place where we can go*
> *as we are and not be questioned.*
> **—MAYA ANGELOU,** *All God's Children Need Traveling Shoes*

Herman Hesse, German poet and philosopher writes:

> *A longing to wander tears my heart when I hear*
> *trees rustling in the wind at evening. If one listens*
> *to them silently for a long time, this longing*
> *reveals its kernel, its meaning. It is not so much a*
> *matter of escaping from one's suffering, though it*
> *may seem to be so. It is a longing for home ... It*
> *leads home. Every path leads homeward.*
> **—HERMAN HESSE,** *Bäume. Betrachtungen und Gedichte*

We long to wander. We seek out wild and exotic places in order to find ourselves — and yet it seems, we also look for our way home. We attempt to both lose and simultaneously find ourselves, in nature, in music, in travel. We desire new views and new experience, looking for a break in sense-dulling routine. We may even distract ourselves in less healthy ways in order to find our way to a place where we feel peace of mind. Where is this place? What is this peace of mind for which we search, this in-between place where we are neither getting away from the "stick" of the past nor chasing the "carrot" of the future? Who is this self we sometimes look for and at other times prefer to lose? What is left when we find our way to a meditative state in which we are able to "vacate"? Some will say that this is where the sacred lies, that this is where the wanderer and the gypsy meet the pilgrim and the Holy Day Maker:

> *Being a pilgrim is a state of mind; it has nothing to do with actual travel. Travelling is symbolic. We travel in life. All of life is a journey.... A pilgrim is someone who sees life as a sacred journey...*
>
> **—SATISH KUMAR,** *Earth Pilgrim*

For others the thought of "vacating" suggests an abandonment and emptiness, or an endless boredom that can be frightening. Letting go of yesterday's expectations and our concerns about tomorrow can be alarming, bringing an unfamiliar and unwelcome vertiginous freedom. Practicing the art of doing nothing for many of us brings self-judgment, so accustomed we are to keeping busy and filling that "unforgiving minute." Others will tell us it is here in this state of surrender that we can feel most present, most alive and at peace. Once we are on the plane after the preparations and the final rush of packing, there is no more to do except to sit back and relax. This surrender to what is happening now, around us, is the beginning of our Holy Day.

As we travel, we have the opportunity to sit back again and again, to relax, leaving the familiar behind so that we can look through fresh eyes at each view, whether new or old, without judgement. What we see then, for the first time, or the fresh time, may be transformed into gold with no further action on our part.

Mountain Magic

On one of the days during a week of guided walks for groups of hikers, we would take the path down to the Cares river from Oceño, a small village 505 metres above sea level with a population in 2016 of just forty-seven souls. After being driven up a steep and winding road with breath-stopping bends and dizzying drops, we visited the cheese caves, followed by a tour of the cheese "factory," a small family business protected by the local *denominación de origen* for the famous Cabrales cheese. The white-knuckled thrill of the drive, the damp musty darkness of the caves, the sharp smell of souring milk in the little room crowded with so many of us, the explanation of the cheesemaking process first in Spanish followed by a rough translation for our visitors — could strain the skittish senses.

Then we stepped out, expanding ourselves once more into alpine meadows, into mountain silence and a magical stillness. We took long breaths of the sense-soothing calm while tall asphodels in bloom reached like quiet white sentinels for the clouds and two birds of prey circled above us in a limitless sky, so close you could hear the rush of air between the feathers of their wings. The swish of those wings, the reverence of words spoken softly between hikers, all this against the backdrop of the palpable yet indescribable serenity of mountain majesty. How can you tell the story when words only point towards what the senses experience?

By the time we reached the riverbank for our picnic lunch and for a *café solo* or a cool drink afterwards at the little bar in Trescares, the magic of that sacred stillness had dimmed behind the sounds of cars on the road, provisions being delivered, neighbours in conversation and dogs dreaming in the sun. I hear that mountain's silence still, while the chatter of the everyday on the road and by the river have long since faded.

When we "read the air" between the spoken words of language, we find ourselves in an intermission between acts, more aware of those around us and more aware of the space and the silence within ourselves. A quiet detachment helps us to hear the sounds and to notice what we may otherwise miss.

Being present for our journeys, whether far afield or close to home, enables us to let go of expectations. We begin to relish the enjoyment of "what is" instead of regretting what wasn't or being concerned about what may not be.

The feelings of aliveness and peace that surface when we are in this place of awareness are the indications that we are following the right path.

> *There arose at once, almost like heartbreak, the memory of Joy itself, the knowledge that I had once had what I had now lacked for years, that I was returning at last from exile and desert lands to my own country.*
> —C.S. LEWIS, *Surprised by Joy*

In this space, gratitude arises unbeckoned, for the days away, for our safe return home and for the ever-unfolding mystery of the present moment. Here, without the chatter of our own noisy thoughts, we may feel calm in a satiated stillness.

> *You have to transcend, or go beyond, the constant activity that fills the mind, like the noise of a radio that cannot be turned off. Beyond that distraction lies a silent region that appears as empty as the quantum field between the stars. Yet like that quantum field, our inner silence holds rich promise.*
> —DEEPAK CHOPRA, *Perfect Health*

Silence and Stillness

I AM MY silence. I am not the busyness of my thoughts or the daily rhythm of my actions. I am not the stuff that constitutes my world. I am not my talk. I am not my actions. I am my silence. I am the consciousness that perceives all these things. When I go to my consciousness, to that great pool of silence that observes the intricacies of my life, I am aware that I am me. I take a little time each day to sit in silence so that I can move outward in balance into the great clamour of living.

—**RICHARD WAGAMESE,** *Embers*

Stillness

Not even birds breach the air, and there rises within you the notion that stillness is more enriching than motion, listening is more empowering than distraction and slow, measured steps feel more graceful than speed.

—**RICHARD WAGAMESE,** *Embers*

Through such stillness and inner quiet, we may uncover the treasure that has been there all the time, the gold reputed to be found in silence.

Rather than a frightening emptiness or an unwelcome freedom, this awareness can bring us new opportunities to see creative potential, wrapped in feelings of enjoyment:

> *In the silence of our minds lies*
> *creative incubation, bringing the*
> *wisdom and the joy we all seek.*
>
> **—SYDNEY BANKS,** *The Missing Link*

Kenny Werner, jazz pianist, speaks about an endless potential for creativity to be found in an "ocean of consciousness, an ocean of bliss":

> *As we expand our limited selves into this infinite*
> *consciousness, we tap into a network of infinite*
> *possibilities, infinite creativity — great, great*
> *power.*
>
> **—KENNY WERNER,** *Effortless Mastery*

In his book about the value of improvisation in life and in art, Stephen Nachmanovitch, improvisational violinist, speaks about this same energy without limit which is the source for all creative activities, and brings in its wake the joy of making art in its many varied forms. He asks:

What then is this seemingly endless stream of music, dance, imagery, acting or speech that comes out of us whenever we let it be? ... We sense something else beyond the personal, from a source that is both very old and very new. The raw material is a kind of flow ... Mysteriously flowing through, unstoppable and unstartable. At its source, it does not appear or disappear, does not increase or decrease, is neither tainted nor pure. We can choose to tap into it or not to tap into it ... it's always there.

—STEPHEN NACHMANOVITCH, Free Play

Is this what we are ultimately searching for, both in our quest for adventure, for the unknown, and in our yearning for the comfort of the familiar and the certainty of home? If it is this flow of joy-filled energy, this creative clay that we seek, then we need look no further as it is already within:

There is a wisdom inside us. There is a spirit inside us. There is an aliveness inside us. It is the intelligence of the universe itself, and we are made of it. When we let it come through us fully, it expresses everywhere.

—MICHAEL NEILL,
"A Daily Dose of Caffeine for the Soul"

Dancing Alone

I remember as a child wearing a new yellow one-piece bathing suit. Stitched to stretch as far as its accordion creases would allow, to expand with my growing frame, it had a frill of a skirt attached at the waist and was the costume of magic and all things possible. I loved it and wearing it I felt like a fairy dressed in gold. I remember dancing without shame or embarrassment around the garden, feeling that I might at any moment take to my wings and fly.

Later, with a room of my own and a pair of pink ballet slippers, I imagined being able to teach myself to dance, practising behind closed doors, until one day I would emerge in unexpected, ecstatic dance.

Many years after that, as a self-conscious teenager, I recall coming home from university and dancing alone in my room in an empty house, no audience, no mirror, just me, feeling only the joy of moving to music and grateful that I had the house to myself.

It is by "some alchemy," writes Nachmanovitch, that

we drop into direct mystic participation in
aliveness or being itself, which is beyond emotion,
skills, thought or imagination... but when we
experience it, it is beyond any doubt.
—STEPHEN NACHMANOVITCH, Free Play

As we become more beguiled by our concepts of separateness, as we gather more years of experience of life, we can search in vain for this vibrant aliveness outside ourselves, in travel, in wild places, in far-off lands and in adventure. Yet what we are looking for is the gold that is already within.

Alchemy

Alchemy is both an art and a science, incorporating a spiritual world view, dating back four millennia and practiced in Europe, China, Africa and Asia. Common to each iteration is the understanding that everything contains a universal spirit. Alchemy is both a mystical philosophy regarding the nature of reality and a scientific method of transmutation by which anything can be reunited with its divine or original form.

Alchemists sought the solution to perfection in the material world through chemical means. They looked for the purification and immortality of the human body and soul through their search for the elixir of life, in Europe often called The Philosopher's Stone (in fact a liquid, powder or wax with magical properties). Their attempts to transform common metals into "noble" metals were based on their belief that all metals were not only alive but also growing inside the earth. Lead for example was thought to simply be a spiritually and physically immature form of a higher metal such as gold:

> To the alchemists, metals were not the unique substances that populate the Periodic Table, but instead the same thing in different stages of development or refinement on their way to spiritual perfection.
> **—BENJAMIN RADFORD, "What is Alchemy?"**

Since gold with its perfect balance of the four elements of fire, air, water and earth symbolized the highest development in metals, it also personified human renewal and regeneration:

A "golden" human being was resplendent with spiritual beauty and had triumphed over the lurking power of evil. The basest metal, lead, represented the sinful and unrepentant individual who was readily overcome by the forces of darkness...

—BENJAMIN RADFORD, "What is Alchemy?"

By changing the proportions of the constituent elements, alchemists believed lead could be transformed into gold. The sought-after Philosopher's Stone, in addition to transforming metals was reputed to be capable of healing all ills, prolonging life, leading to immortality and was the ultimate reconnection to the divine.

While its association with philosophy, religion and magic is apparent, alchemy is also considered the precursor to modern chemistry and medicine including the development of laboratory techniques and the experimental method. Sir Isaac Newton, more famous for his understanding of gravity and the laws governing motion, also wrote copiously on the subject.

Alchemy continues to influence literature and the arts.

In the flow of creative exploration, we find the treasure for which many travel the world:

When the muse is full upon you, you move to the chair at your desk as if entranced, and in that ghostly glow against the full dark before sunrise, story becomes a shape-shifter, a presence that cajoles you, tempts you, coaxes words to eke out onto the page, creating worlds and people from the fire deep within you so that this alchemy of creation becomes transcendent, making time lose all its properties. There is just you and the universe and this creative fire moving through your fingers in bold palettes of colour chasing the dark away until you emerge in the sure, calm light of morning and feel like a writer again.

—**RICHARD WAGAMESE,** *Embers*

Dancing the Zeibekiko

On the same trip to Greece mentioned earlier, I spent an evening in the Plaka district of ancient Athens as the guest of the hotel receptionist. He told me with pride and conviction and few words in English that in Greece "we have everything — your discotheques and our own Greek nightclubs." We visited both. The discotheque was loud and crowded, no room for free movement and a volume that prevented any conversation we might have had. At the Greek nightclub there were glasses of water on the counter at the bar and there was no cover charge. As the music played, several of the men arose from their seats. One by one, each took his turn, including my companion. Without a word, with absolute certainty and complete assurance, he danced. Slender and enraptured, he danced alone. I felt honoured to witness such freedom of expression in someone I hardly knew. With his limited English, he remained silent and I, from shyness and with decorum, did not interrupt. When it was time to go, he delivered me safely back to the hotel where I was staying.

Yes, they had it all, the changing fashion of the day and their traditional direct connection to life itself, felt but unspoken, unclouded by inhibition in its blissful unselfconsciousness.

The *Zeibekiko*

It is difficult to dance the *Zeibekiko*. There are no set steps, no particular rhythm, only the repetition of a circular motion. It requires

> an inner intensity, because it is an improvised movement that expresses the feelings of the individual who gets up to dance.
>
> **—PHILIP CHRYSOPOULOS,**
> **"The History and Tradition of the Greek Dance Zeibekiko"**

The name comes from *Zeybeks*, a group of irregular militia and guerilla fighters who lived in the Aegean region of the Ottoman Empire. According to Greek sources they were islamized Greeks. Originally a dance for two armed men facing one another, the *Zeibekiko*, sometimes known as the "eagle dance" because the dancers looked like birds of prey circling, is best known nowadays as an improvised dance for a man dancing alone.

With humility and dignity, the dancer is not embarrassed to show his pain or weaknesses. To dance the *Zeibekiko* is to express "the despair of life, of the unfulfilled dream." The dancer lets his emotions overwhelm him, choses the song he will dance to, alone with his demons, "Like a man who faces the abyss."

Yet "a great *Zeibekiko* dancer is one who looks like they are dancing on clouds."

A man will dance the *Zeibekiko* only once without monopolizing the floor. He does not dance for an audience. He dances for himself.

The *Zeibekiko* is a private, intensely personal moment, like prayer:

> If injustice, love and pain disappear from this world, or if we find another way that men can express their feelings with so much beauty and kindness, then zeibekiko might be lost as well.

—GREEK MUSIC GREEK SONGS,
"A Manly Zeibekiko Dance"

Writers, musicians, artists, shamans and healers have all recognized a transpersonal force that flows through us and all creation, literally in-spiring (breathing into) us.

Ch'i, ki, prana, puhpowee (Potawatomi language) are all words for "the animacy of the world, the life that pulses through all things."

Dancing with Words

Attention, taken to its highest degree, is the same thing as prayer. It presupposes faith and love.
—Simone Weil, *Gravity and Grace*

These two lips like tulips in the garden quietly shout, ready to open wide in an expression of dazzling colour. These fine tulip troops, feeling the warmth of spring sunshine in their hearts will unfurl their tender wings to welcome the admiration of bees and birds. For all of us who are witness to their daily parade of gaudy splendour, they will deliver their message of hope and glory. By night and when soft spring rains fall, they will close, fold in upon themselves so they may rekindle their creative fire. By day they will open once more to display their brilliance while the elasticity of their being permits. Then like others of the brief floral candles in the garden, their time will pass.

Like the tulips I bide my time. Out of silence and stillness I find the words, the words find me.

Like the woodpecker who wakes me now each morning with the sound of his loud pecking on the metal roof. No grubs or bugs to feed him there. He stops, he looks around to see if She has heard. I with the reddest neck, the loudest drum. Are you watching? No shame, no awkwardness, simply awareness of creation. I'm waiting.

The Woman in Red takes to the floor with poise and grace. I'm dancing with words. I'm speaking.

Duende is a Spanish word for which we have no single word translation in English. More often applied to flamenco music and dance, it is also the feeling of awe and inspiration when you stand in nature. It describes those moments in artistic activity when something else takes over, when a "creative fire" speaks through you and you feel an overwhelming sense of beauty and magic. It is the shivers up your spine, the cries of "Olé!", "Allah!", "Viva Dios!" in those who witness creation in the moment of its birth in the music and dance of flamenco. It's similar to the Muse or the Angel, but whereas those come from above, beyond and outside you, *duende* rises up from within.

The word comes from *dueño de casa*, lord or owner of the house, meaning a sort of *dæmon* or local spirit. It also refers to the genius loci, the spirit of place embodied by the nymphs and sprites who live in the forests, beside the streams, wherever we feel the presence of the mystery of nature. It is both "the magic inside yourself, in your soul, that makes you express yourself uniquely" and the awareness of that spirit, charisma, aliveness experienced by others in its presence. It connects us to each other like tuning forks in sympathetic resonance and to the natural world of which we are a part. Here is where journey and destination become one.

> *Beauty as wholeness breaks for a moment the*
> *bonds of limitation which separate artists from*
> *their work and from us. A beautiful work of art*
> *demonstrates and celebrates "inter-being." ...*
> *Beautiful art doesn't so much answer questions*
> *or set agendas as create space — space where we*
> *can laugh and mourn and experience a wider*

and deeper fullness of life in unbroken
communion with the universe.

—**LEONARD BIALLAS,** *Pilgrim*

Beauty, both experienced in the creative fire and witnessed in the created flame, unites the one through whom it passes with the one who observes its passage. It is in this sacred timeless space, whether far afield or at home, where we can experience fulfillment, stillness and silence, surrender and release. Whether as the artist who transforms the invisible into the visible, or the beholder who is its spectator, beauty brings joy.

This whole adventure of creativity is about joy
and love. We live for the pure joy of being, and
out of that joy unfold the ten thousand art forms
and all the branches of learning and
compassionate activity.

—**STEPHEN NACHMANOVITCH,** *Free Play*

As joy and love are the food of music and of art and of all artistic and creative endeavours, so also they may inspire "all the branches of learning and compassionate activity." While we sometimes limit ourselves to thinking that imagination is only the vehicle for artistic creation, making the invisible visible is a much bigger concept. It takes the eye of inner vision, perception beyond ordinary sight, the eye of the heart and of the spirit to visualize what is not yet seen, something new, until now unnamed. In this, the scientist is not different from the artist:

265

*[The scientist] wishes to ... find a certain oneness.
... the artist, the musical composer, the architect,
the scientist all feel a fundamental need to
discover and create something new that is whole
and total, harmonious and beautiful. Few ever
get a chance to try to do this, and even fewer
actually manage to do it. Yet, deep down, it is
probably what very large numbers of people in
all walks of life are seeking when they attempt to
escape the daily humdrum routine by engaging
in every kind of entertainment, excitement,
stimulation, change of occupation, and so forth,
through which they ineffectively try to
compensate for the unsatisfying narrowness and
mechanicalness of their lives.*

—DAVID BOHM, *On Creativity*

Is this then the longing we feel, each of us, as we travel, or
as we stay still, for beauty, for joy, for harmony?

Imaginación

When we moved from Spain our youngest son, feeling nostalgic for the sight of the Picos de Europa mountains and the Mar Cantabrico, described his longing for those views:

"It gave me *imaginación* — now I don't know if I can find it."

"What was that imagination you spoke of? Did you find it again?" I asked him the other day.

"It was a feeling of hope and possibility. Someone told me that from the top of those mountains you could see the wheat fields of Castilla y León. I imagined castles and infinite plains stretching further than my eye could see. It was a feeling of limitless potential. I associate it now with the space in which I can write music. I go there whenever I create, that place of imagination, only now I can find it in other mountains, other views, wherever I am when I see the endless opportunities for beauty."

As sage, Sydney Banks pointed out:

Love is a living, breathing essence that the wise can pluck from the air at will and then like a master artist mold it into something beautiful.

—SYDNEY BANKS, Second Chance

Whether the creative venture is the destination or the journey, whether it is the work of art or our own unique expression of aliveness, a compassionate activity or our openness to adventure and discovery through learning, it is sacred.

The greatest art is the art of love, for all other arts emerge out of the art of love.

—SATISH KUMAR, Earth Pilgrim

This, I believe, is the "thin place" in which we can spend a Holy Day, knowing that we are both simultaneously en route and at home. Here, in a timeless space, wherever we are, is where the veil between the sacred or divine and what we see as every day, ordinary reality, is translucent.

Extreme attention is what constitutes the creative faculty in man and the only extreme attention is religious.

—SIMONE WEIL, Gravity and Grace

La Imaginación
Es Tu Camino de Oro

[Imagination is your path of gold]

He was there perched on the dunes above the beach, the Playa de Papagayo, eyes intent, his focus alternating between the distance and the pad of paper balanced on his lap. Soft charcoal pencil gracefully poised between long first finger and a flexible thumb — he was sketching. He had no idea what lay around the corner or even how long he had been there, because he was immersed in his drawing. Simple, steady traces in pencil, the horizon marked in grey where the sea met the rocks and the sky melted into the sea. Lines drawn with certainty, no hesitation as he saw that view in that moment, no need to retrace his steps, no need to correct the perfection of that moment. With no backwards glance, no thought of the future, he turned to leave. Fully present as he arrived to see the car stuck in the sand ... to see them looking at him as he looked at them. Fully present to enter their stories as they entered his in this time and in this space.

In this journey there is no endpoint,
because it is the journey into the soul.

—STEPHEN NACHMANOVITCH, *Free Play*

After Words

You know who you are, you have taught me so much about holidaymaking. The best recipes for making happy memories you have shared with me — the holiday initiation, jumping into the pool fully clad — holiday traditions — the art of doing nothing when those around you clamour for entertainment and activity — allowing adventure to happen, welcoming the unexpected because it is through getting lost that we discover new places and thereby ourselves. Letting go of the things we usually take for granted — the sheets for the beds when they told us to bring our own — and the inventions you came up with and solutions you always found. Always taking responsibility for our homes away from home and facing every challenge with optimism and humour. We met while both on holiday and for this and the precious happy Holy Days we have shared, I thank you.

Points of Interest

Additional notes that may be useful or interesting are listed with the notes at the end of each chapter.

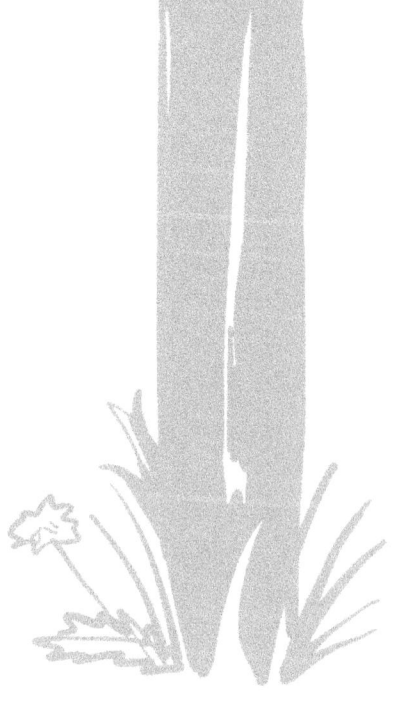

Notes

INTRODUCTION

Point of Interest

It is useful to make outer journeys in order to make inner journeys, but the significant realisation of a pilgrimage is in the consciousness that the whole of the Earth is a sacred site. Of course, every one of us can discover a particular site which resonates with our spirit, where we can go and be in solitude and find ourselves, whether it be a particular tree, or hill, or corner of the seashore. Such special sacred sites can be a significant symbol. In the same way that a mantra is a sound which connects us with the cosmic consciousness, a particular grove, cave or valley can be a point to connect us with the Earth. —Satish Kumar

—Kumar, S. (2009). *Earth pilgrim: Conversations with Satish Kumar.* Green Books / UIT Cambridge, p. 13.

CHAPTER 1
Wanderlust *or* Fernweh?

Weidensaul, S. (1999). *Living on the wind: Across the hemisphere with migratory birds.* North Point Press.

Quinion, M. (2006, October 21). *Gringo.* World Wide Words. https://www.worldwidewords.org/qa/qa-gri1.htm

Montezuma's revenge. (2020, December 20). In *Wiktionary.* https://en.wiktionary.org/wiki/Montezuma%27s_revenge

CHAPTER 2
Schwellenangst *or* Resfeber?

Allen, L. (2019, July 8). Tortilla de patatas. *Tastes Better From Scratch.* https://tastesbetterfromscratch.com/tortilla-de-patatas/

Nawijn, J., Marchand, M. A., Veenhoven, R. & Vingerhoets, A. J. (2010). "Vacationers happier, but most not happier after a holiday." *Applied Research Quality Life, 5,* 35–47. https://doi.org/10.1007/s11482-009-9091-9

Gilovich, T., Kumar, A., & Jampol, L. (2014). A wonderful life: experiential consumption and the pursuit of happiness. *Journal of Consumer Psychology, 25*(1). http://dx.doi.org/10.1016/j.jcps.2014.08.004)

U.S. Travel Association. (2019, August 16). *Study: A record 768 million U.S. vacation days went unused in '18, opportunity cost in the billions.* https://www.ustravel.org/press/study-record-768-million-us-vacation-days-went-unused-18-opportunity-cost-billions

Gatayama, M. (2018, December 18). Japanese workers take only half their paid vacation, survey finds. *Nikkei Asia.* https://asia.nikkei.com/Business/Business-trends/Japanese-workers-take-only-half-their-paid-vacation-survey-finds

Miller, K. (n.d.) 50 examples of funny out of office messages that are hilarious and creative. *Future of Working.* Retrieved March 1, 2020, from https://futureofworking.com/50-examples-of-funny-out-of-office-messages-that-are-hilarious-and-creative

Watson, J. (2016, June 7). Out of the ordinary out-of-office replies. Core24. https://core24.com/out-of-the-ordinary-out-of-office-replies

CHAPTER 3
Travelling Light

Sharkey, J. (2010, October 4). *Reinventing the suitcase by adding the wheel.* The New York Times. https://www.nytimes.com/-2010/10/05/business/05road.html

Point of Interest

American inventor, Bernard Sadow is credited with the invention of the wheeled suitcase in 1970, but a photo taken in 1954 of Polish artist, Alfred Krupa shows him with his home-made wheeled luggage nearly 20 years earlier.

Chatham, N. (2020, February 26). Was suitcase on wheels invented by Pole? New photo shows artist Alfred Krupa with iconic suitcase nearly 20 years BEFORE idea was patented by US inventor. The First News. https://www.thefirstnews.com/-article/was-suitcase-on-wheels-invented-by-pole-new-photo-shows-artist-alfred-krupa-with-iconic-suitcase-nearly-20-years -before-idea-was-patented-by-us-inventor-10720

CHAPTER 4
Bon Voyage

Werner, K. (1996). *Effortless Mastery: Liberating the Master Musician Within.* Jamey Aebersold Jazz, p. 11.

Points of Interest

For me a flight is just a brief retreat in the sky. There's nothing I can do, so it's really quite liberating. There's nowhere else I can be. So I just sit and watch the clouds and the blue sky. Everything is still and everything is moving. It's beautiful. —Scientist and monk, Matthieu Ricard, in response to the question, how did he deal with jet lag?

—Iyer, P. (2014). *The Art of Stillness: Adventures in Going Nowhere.* Simon & Schuster/ TED, pp. 25–26.

The truest and most horrible claim made for modern transport is that it "annihilates space." It does. It annihilates one of the most glorious gifts we have been given. It is a vile inflation which lowers the value of distance, so that a modern boy travels a hundred miles with less sense of liberation and pilgrimage and adventure than his grandfather got from travelling ten. —C.S. Lewis

—Lewis, C. S. (1955). *Surprised by Joy: The Shape of my Early Life.* Harcourt Brace, pp. 150–151.

CHAPTER 5
Place or Time Travel?

Stringfellow, K., (2020, June). *Bringing creation back together again: The Salt Songs of the Nuwuvi.* The Mojave Project. https://mojaveproject.org/dispatches-item/bringing-creation-back-together-again-the-salt-songs-of-the-nuwuvi/

Kimmerer, R. W. (2013). *Braiding Sweetgrass: Indigenous Wisdom, Scientific Knowledge and the Teachings of Plants.* Milkweed Editions, p. 17.

Carman, W. B., & Hovey, R. (1894). *Songs from Vagabondia.* Copeland & Day.

Graburn, N. H. H. (1989). Tourism: The sacred journey. In V. L. Smith (Ed.), *Hosts and Guests: The Anthropology of Tourism* (pp. 19–36). https://doi.org/10.9783/9780812208016.19

Ponder, A. J. (2010, September 20). *"My Mother Said...Anonymous."* An Affliction of Poetry. https://anafflictionofpoetry.blogspot.com/2010/09/my-mother-said-anonymous.html

Why are Romani called Romani? What is their link with the Romans if there is one? (2015). In *Reddit.* https://www.reddit.com/r/AskHistorians/comments/2f5o6o/why_are_romani_called_romani_what_is_their_link/

Carella, D. From an interview with Laurel Victoria Gray. By permission of the author.

Cher, (1971). "Gypsies, Tramps, and Thieves." [Song] *On Gypsys, Tramps & Thieves.* Kapp Records; MCA.

Conger, C., (2009). *How Gypsies work.* Howstuffworks. http://people.howstuffworks.com/gypsy5.htm

Gray, L. G. (1996). *Gypsy in their souls: The West preserves Gypsy dance traditions.* The Best of Habibi. http://thebestofhabibi.com/vol-15-no-1-winter-1996/gypsy-in-their-souls/

CHAPTER 6
Bienvenue: *The Enchantment of Arrival*

Wacks, D. A. (2014, December 12). *Some Thoughts on Asturian Mythology*. Research and Teaching on Medieval Iberian and Sephardic Culture. https://davidwacks.uoregon.edu/2014/12/12/asturian/

Smith, V. L. (Ed.). (1978). *Hosts and Guests: The Anthropology of Tourism*. University of Pennsylvania Press, p. 1. https://doi.org/10.9783/9780812208016

Pollan, M. (2018). *How to Change your Mind: What the New Science of Psychedelics Teaches Us About Consciousness, Dying, Addiction, Depression, and Transcendence*. Penguin Press, p. 16.

Point of Interest

Despite all the identifying, measuring, photographing, I had managed to set the experience in a kind of present past, a having looked, even as I was temporally and physically still looking...It is not necessarily too little knowledge that causes ignorance; possessing too much, or wanting to gain too much, can produce the same result. —**John Fowles, The Tree**

—Fowles, J. (1979). *The Tree*, Little, Brown.

CHAPTER 7
Perfection, Completion and the Lure of Familiarity

Bethune, A. (2013). Introduction. In *Musicpreneur: The Creative Approach to Making Money in Music*. Above the Noise.

Treadway, D. & Treadway, K. (n.d.). *About the Innkeepers*. Log Cabin Inn. https://www.kenorabedandbreakfast.com/

Nick & Neda. (2021). *About Us*. The Orange Bicycle. https://www.orangebicyclebnb.com/AboutUs.html

Bethune, *Musicpreneur*, p. 5.

Point of Interest

> Wabi-Sabi *is the Japanese concept of the acceptance of transience and imperfection and the awareness of the beauty in incompletion and impermanence. When we are reminded that all things — and life itself, are transient, we are more inclined to enjoy the moment, appreciating what is in front of us.*

CHAPTER 8
Pan del Dia: *The Currency of Language and the Language of Currency*

Nachmanovitch, S. (1993). *Free Play: Improvisation in Life and Art.* Penguin-Tarcher, p. 9.

Meyer, E. (2016). *The Culture Map: Breaking Through the Invisible Boundaries of Global Busines*s, p. 37.

Turner, J. (2020, January 21*). 'Reading the air' in Japanese culture.* Japan Insider. https://japaninsider.com/reading-the-air/

Bylund, E., & Athanasopoulos, P. (2017, July). The Whorfian time warp: Representing duration through the language hourglass. *Journal of Experimental Psychology. General, 146*(7), 911–916. http://doi:org/10.1037/xge0000314

Kimmerer, *Braiding Sweetgrass*, p. 55.

Grabianowski, E. (n.d). *How Currency Works: How Stuff Works.* https://money.howstuffworks.com/currency.htm

Banknote World (2016, July 26). *10 of the World's Most Unique Currency.* https://www.banknoteworld.com/blog/10-of-the-worlds-most-unique-currency/

Points of Interest

> *Those in whom the Greek word lives only while they are hunting for it in the lexicon, and who then substitute the English word for it, are not reading the Greek at all; they are only solving a puzzle.*

The very formula, "Naus means a ship," is wrong. Naus and ship both mean a thing, they do not mean one another. Behind Naus, as behind navis or naca, we want to have a picture of a dark, slender mass with sail or oars, climbing the ridges, with no officious English word intruding. —**C.S. Lewis**

—Lewis, *Surprised by Joy*, p. 115.

In Northern Kurdish language (Kurmanji), the same word can have two genders according to the context. For example, if the word dar (meaning wood or tree) is feminine, it means that it is a living tree (e.g. dara sêvê means "apple tree"), but if it is masculine, it means that it is dead, no longer living (e.g. darê sêvê means "apple wood"). So if one wants to refer to a certain table that is made of wood from an apple tree, one cannot use the word dar with a feminine gender, and if one wants to refer to an apple tree in a garden, one cannot use dar with a masculine gender. — **Wikipedia**

—Grammatical gender. (2021, June 21). In Wikipedia. https://en.wikipedia.org/wiki/Grammatical_gender

In Japanese, using the existential verbs "Iru" for animate and "Aru" for inanimate objects is a simple way of distinguishing between animacy and inanimacy.

CHAPTER 9
Guidebooks, Maps and Getting Lost

Vive El Camino. (n.d.). *The codex calixtinus.* https://vivecamino.com/en/the-pilgrimage/the-codex-calixtinus/

Carroll, L. (1893). *Sylvie and Bruno Concluded. Vol. 11.* Gutenberg EBook. p. 169.

Kher, S. (2014, August 21). *On the Consequences of a One to One Scale Map*. Rapid Uplift. http://suvratk.blogspot.com/2014/08/on-consequences-of-one-to-one-scale-map.html

The Cultural Conservancy (n.d.). *The salt song trail project*. http://www.nativeland.org/salt-song-trail

Moat, J. (1991). The resurgence bark. *Resurgence & Ecologist, 148*, 2.

Global Positioning System. (2021, February 4). In *Wikipedia*. https://en.wikipedia.org/wiki/Global_Positioning_System

Richey, M. W., Howard, J. L., May, W. E., Jones, S. S. D., Logsdon, T. S., & Anderson, E. W. (2021, January 29). Navigation. *Encyclopedia Britannica*. https://www.britannica.com/technology/navigation-technology

Rodgers, A. C. (2013, December 3). Compass. *National Geographic*. www.nationalgeographic.org/encyclopedia/compass/

Chronometer watch. (January 24, 2021). In *Wikipedia*. https://en.wikipedia.org/wiki/Chronometer_watch

Chang, K. (2004, June 1). "Constant as the North Star? More like fickle." *The New York Times*. http://www.nytimes.com/-2004/06/01/health/constant-as-the-north-star-more-like-fickle.html

Britannica. (n.d.). Navigation. In *Britannica.com dictionary*. Retrieved February 23, 2021, from https://www.britannica.com/technology/navigation-technology

Debord, Guy. (March 4, 2021). In *Wikipedia*. https://en.wikipedia.org/wiki/Guy_Debord

The Adventure Diary (2016, November 4). *Why you should coddiwomple your way through life*. https://adventurediary.co/coddiwomple-definition/

So, W. (2017, July 12). *Travel Makes us Happy: Here's Why.* CNN Travel. www.cnn.com/travel/article/travel-makes-us-happy/index.html

Nachmanovitch, *Free Play,* p. 19.

Berry, W. (1982). Our real work. *Standing by Words: Essays.* Counterpoint.

May, R. (1969). *Love and Will.* W. W. Norton & Company, p. 15.

Solnit, R. (2005). *A field guide to getting lost.* Penguin Books, p. 6.

Thoreau, H.D. (1854). *Walden; or, Life in the Woods.* Beacon Press, p. 162.

Points of Interest

Polish-American scientist and philosopher Alfred Korzybski remarked that "the map is not the territory" and that "the word is not the thing," encapsulating his view that an abstraction derived from something, or a reaction to it, is not the thing itself. Korzybski held that many people do confuse maps with territories, that is, confuse models of reality with reality itself. The relationship has also been expressed in other terms, such as Alan Watts's "The menu is not the meal." —**Wikipedia**

—Map-territory relation. (2021, January 9). In *Wikipedia.* https://en.wikipedia.org/wiki/Map%E2%80%93territory_relation

I've had a preliminary look for evidence for a verb coddiwomple, and the earliest conventional printed sources I can find it in are newspapers from August and September last year, although it does seem to appear somewhat earlier online, in blogs and the like. It doesn't appear in any of our dictionaries of regional English, such as the English Dialect Dictionary or the Dictionary of American Regional English, and I can't find it in the major dictionaries of slang either, although that may be because it's too recent.

I am slightly suspicious that almost all occurrences of coddiwomple give it the same definition word for word, rather than simply using the verb in a natural sentence, which suggests to me that this may be a relatively recent invention which has caught on to a certain extent online. That doesn't make it any less of a "real word" necessarily, but for the OED's purposes, it's probably a little too recent for us to include at the moment, unless more evidence comes to light. We like to be sure that a word is properly established in the English language with a reasonable amount of currency before we include it in the OED. —Simone, "Coddiwomple"

—Simone (2017, December). Coddiwomple [Online forum post]. *Oxford Living Dictionaries.* https://forum.oxforddictionaries.com/en/discussion/12/-coddiwomple

CHAPTER 10
Mono No Aware: *The Beauty of Transience*

Pasteur, L. (1854, December 7). *Dans les champs de l'observation le hasard ne favorise que les esprits préparés* [In the fields of observation chance favours only the prepared mind] [Lecture]. University of Lille, France.

Gilovich, T., Kumar, A., & Jampol, L. (2014). A wonderful life: experiential consumption and the pursuit of happiness. *Journal of Consumer Psychology, 25*(1), 155–156.

Tonks, L. (2018, January 18). *Most popular souvenirs.* Icelolly.com. https://www.icelolly.com/blog/most-popular-souvenirs

Prusinski, L. (2013). *Wabi sabi, mono no aware, and ma: Tracing traditional Japanese aesthetics through Japanese history.* Semantic Scholar, p. 28. https://www.semanticscholar.org/paper/Wabi-Sabi%2C-Mono-no-Aware%2C-and-Ma%3A-Tracing-Japanese-Prusinski/9719f684a62fe7d9d43457042a600fb56978793b

Point of Interest

"Wand'rin' Star" is a song that was originally written for the stage musical Paint Your Wagon in 1951. When the film of the musical was made in 1969, Lee Marvin took the role of prospector Ben Rumson. Not a natural singer, Marvin nevertheless sang all of his songs in the film, rejecting the idea of miming to another singer's voice. Although the film was a box office failure, the soundtrack became a success. Marvin's version of the song "Wand'rin' Star" was a number-one single in Ireland and the UK. Marvin never released a follow-up single, so he is considered a "one-hit wonder."
—**Wikipedia**

—"Wand'rin' Star." (2021, January 31). In *Wikipedia.*
https://en.wikipedia.org/wiki/Wand'rin'_Star

CHAPTER 11
Mushin: *The Art of Vacating*

Nawijn et al., "Vacationers happier."

Kipling, R. (1943). "If," *A Choice of Kipling's Verse.* The Poetry Foundation. https://www.poetryfoundation.org/poems/-46473/if

Iyer, *The Art of Stillness*, p. 62.

Coelho, P. (2011, November 6). *Paolo Coelho on Santiago de Compostela.* Newsweek. https://www.newsweek.com/paolo-coelho-santiago-de-compostela-66335

Points of Interest

The Alchemist is about Santiago, an Andalusian shepherd boy who travels from his home to the Egyptian desert in quest of a treasure he has been told in a dream is buried near the Pyramids. The story tells of his meetings with a Gypsy woman, a man who calls himself king, and an alchemist, all of whom point Santiago in the direction of his search. What starts out as a journey to find gold turns into the realization of the treasure found within, symbolized by Santiago's discovery of a chest of gold and jewels buried under the very tree where he had his prophetic dream.

—Coelho, P. (1993). *The Alchemist* (A. R. Clarke, Trans.). HarperOne. (Original work published 1988)

The Law of Resonance – more information:

—Physics Classroom. (2021). *Forced Vibration.* https://www.physicsclassroom.com/class/sound/Lesson-4/Forced-Vibration

More on the February Butterfly:

If it had once eluded me by its distance, it now eluded me by proximity—something too near to see, too plain to be understood, on this side of knowledge. It seemed to have been always with me; if I could ever have turned my head quick enough I should have seized it. Now for the first time I felt that it was out of reach not because of something I could not do but because of something I could not stop doing. If I could only leave off, let go, unmake myself, it would be there. —**C.S. Lewis**

Lewis, *Surprised by Joy*, p. 170.

Let your mind be still, for the wisdom you seek is like that butterfly over yonder. If you try and catch it with your intellect, it will simply fly away. On the other hand, if you can still your mind, some day when you least expect it, it will land on the palm of your hand. —**Sydney Banks**

Banks, S. (2001). *The Enlightened Gardener,* Lone Pine Publishing, p. 111.

CHAPTER 12
Saudade: *Sweet Sorrow*

Eliot, T.S. (1942). "Little Gidding", No. 4 of *Four Quartets*.

Facebook post (2020, February). Permission to quote granted by author.

Hammond, C. (2012). *Time Warped: Unlocking the Mysteries of Time Perception*, pp. 197–98. Harper Perennial.

Solomon, A. (2013, April 25). "This too shall pass: Tracing an ancient Jewish folktale." *Medium*. https://medium.com/-learning-for-life/this-too-shall-pass-tracing-an-ancient-jewish-folktale-6f5a1aaa0a0e

Shakespeare, W. (1594). *Romeo and Juliet*, 2.2.

Celine Da Costa. (2021, March 9). Words beyond translation: Saudade. *Rosetta Stone.* https://blog.rosettastone.com/words-beyond-translation-saudade/

Solnit, *A Field Guide to Getting Lost*, p. 23.

CHAPTER 13
Sehnsucht: Longing for Time Past

Bunyan, J. (1885). *The Pilgrim's Progress from this World, to that Which is to Come*. Belford, Clarke & Company.

Chesterton, G.K. (1909). "The riddle of the ivy". *Tremendous Trifles: A Collection of Essays*.

Wagamese, R. (2016). *Embers: One Ojibway's Meditations*, Douglas & McIntyre, p. 170. Reproduced by permission of the publisher.

Iyer, *The Art of Stillness*, p. 14.

Lewis, *Surprised by Joy*, p. 24.

Solnit, *A Field Guide to Getting Lost*, p. 30.

Friends of Silence. (2002, January). *Home is within you: Thich Nhat Hanh.* https://friendsofsilence.net/quote/2002/01/home-within-you

Post-vacation blues. (2020, October 17). In *Wikipedia.* https://en.wikipedia.org/wiki/Post-vacation_blues

U.S. Travel Association. (2015, February 3). *U.S. Travel Announces reimagined initiative — Project: Time Off.* https://www.ustravel.org/press/us-travel-announces-reimagined-initiative-project-time

Achor, S. (2015, June 12). Are the people who take vacations the ones who get promoted? *Harvard Business Review.* https://hbr.org/2015/06/are-the-people-who-take-vacations-the-ones-who-get-promoted

Point of Interest

Achor, S. (2011, May). *The happy secret to better work* [Video]. TED Conferences. https://www.ted.com/talks/shawn_achor_the_happy_secret_to_better_work?

CHAPTER 14
Armchair Travels: A Pilgrim's Mindset

Santayana, G. (1995). The philosophy of travel. In D. Cory (Ed.), *The Birth of Reason and Other Essays.* Columbia University Press. (Original work published 1968), p. 15.

The Seattle School. (2018, April 10). *Alumni spotlight: Mary DeJong and Waymarkers.* https://theseattleschool.edu/blog/alumni-mary-dejong-waymarkers/

See Point of Interest Chapter 11 for a plot summary of *The Alchemist.*

Biallas, L. (2002). *Pilgrim: A spirituality of travel.* Franciscan Press. p. 23.

Kimmerer, *Braiding Sweetgrass*, p. 296, 300.

Carlsen, S. (2020). *A Walk Around the Block: Stoplight Secrets, Mischievous Squirrels, Manhole Mysteries and Other Stuff You See Every Day (and Know Nothing About).* HarperCollins.

Horowitz, A. (2014). *On Looking: Eleven walks with Expert Eyes.* Simon & Schuster, p. 2. By permission of the author.

Viator. (2021). *Virtual tours around the world.* https://www.viator.com/collections/virtual-tours-around-the-world/c148

Kipling, "If," *A Choice of Kipling's Verse.*

Solomon, This too shall pass.

Days Of The Year (2021). Retrieved October 25, 2021, from https://www.daysoftheyear.com/

Point of Interest

To see a world in a grain of sand, and a heaven in a wild flower.
To hold infinity in the palm of your hand, and eternity in an hour.
—William Blake, "Auguries of Innocence"

—Blake, W. *Auguries of Innocence.* Poetry Foundation https://www.poetryfoundation.org/poems/43650/auguries-of-innocence

CHAPTER 15
Duende: *The Alchemy of Home*

Angelou, M. (1986). *All God's Children Need Traveling Shoes.* Random House, p. 166.

Hesse, H. (1972). *Bäume. Betrachtungen und Gedichte [Wandering; Notes and Sketches]* (James Wright, Trans.) Straus & Giroux. (Original work published in 1920).

Kumar, *Earth Pilgrim*, p. 107.

Kipling, "If," *A Choice of Kipling's Verse.*

Lewis, *Surprised by Joy*, p. 75.

Chopra, D. (1990). *Perfect Health: The Complete Mind/Body Guide*, Bantam Books, p. 16.

Wagamese, *Embers*, p. 15, 26.

Banks, S. (2018). *The Missing link: Reflections on Philosophy and Spirit*, Lone Pine Publishing, p.9

Werner, *Effortless Mastery*, p. 13.

Nachmanovitch, *Free Play*, p. 32.

Neill, M. (2020, December 7). *A daily dose of caffeine for the soul.* https://www.michaelneill.org/caffeine-for-the-soul/

Nachmanovitch, *Free Play*, p. 173.

Radford, B. (n.d.). What is alchemy? *Live Science.* https://www.livescience.com/39314-alchemy.html

Wagamese, *Embers,* p. 52.

Chrysopoulos, P. (2021, March 2). *The History and Tradition of the Greek Dance Zeibekiko.* Greek Reporter. https://greekreporter.com/2021/03/02/history-tradition-greek-zeibekiko-dance/

Greek Music Greek Songs. (n.d.). *A Manly Zeibekiko Dance.* https://www.greeksongs-greekmusic.com/manly-zeibekiko-dance/

Kimmerer, *Braiding Sweetgrass*, p. 55.

Weil, S. (2021). *Gravity and Grace.* [Kindle version], p. 114.

Definition of *duende*: personal communication, September 2020.

Biallas, *Pilgrim*, pp. 137–138.

Nachmanovitch, *Free Play*, pp. 165–166.

Bohm, D. (2004). *On Creativity*. [Kindle version], p. 3.

Banks, S. (1983). *Second Chance*. Pine Mountain Press, p. 86.

Kumar, *Earth Pilgrim*, p. 81.

Points of Interest

> *We are all searching for our home grounds. We're searching to find the way home. And to find the way home, what we have to do is look at everything in reverse, because naturally if you're away from home, if you keep walking you walk further away. To find home you've got to turn around. You have got to go the opposite and instead of searching outside for the answer you seek, all you do is turn around and look inside. And there lie the secrets that you want.* —Sydney Banks

—Banks, S. (n.d.) "Best of two worlds" [Audio recording episode]. In *A Collection of Four Vintage Recordings*. IHRC

In another book, Robin Wall Kimmerer explains *puhpowee*:

> *we are all connected by our common understanding of the calls filling the night at the start of spring. It is the wordless voice of longing that resonates within us, the longing to continue, to participate in the sacred life of the world.* —Robin Wall Kimmerer

—Kimmerer, R. W. (2003). *Gathering Moss: A Natural and Cultural History of Mosses*. Oregon State University Press, p. 28.

After Words

Nachmanovitch, *Free Play*, p. 11.

About the Author

The author started travelling young, on a family holiday to France when she was three. A vaguely remembered glimpse of a black wrought-iron balcony and the Mediterranean blue beyond may be fantasy rather than memory. Family hiking holidays in the French Alps awakened her love for the mountains. Her first solo trip and flight was when she was twelve, to be met in Geneva by a French family with whom she spent the next three weeks, in theory to learn the language and in practice to taste the subtly, indescribably different ways in which we live our lives.

Since then she has travelled for fun, for adventure, for education, for work and for love.

She spent the first thirteen years of her life in England before moving to Montréal, Canada, with her family. She completed high school and then spent two and a half years in Switzerland. After attending two universities in Ontario, she returned once more to the UK for a master's degree in literature. She lived in Ontario and in British Columbia for six years then came back to Montréal where she completed a degree and a half in Social Work. After all this travelling around she moved back to England where she stayed still for nearly six years before meeting a special Swedish someone on a beach in the Canary Islands. They moved to Spain and ran a small hotel in the Picos de Europa Mountains in northern Spain for thirteen years. From there they emigrated back to British Columbia with their sons, and she began a program for the local school district called "Connecting Generations."

Sarah has moved between continents three times, between countries four times and she has lived in four different Canadian provinces. During the pandemic, she drove across the country. She currently resides in Nova Scotia on the Atlantic coast of Canada where she has opened a B&B.

Despite suffering from car sickness as a child, she continues to find stillness in motion. She is grateful for the many opportunities she has had to experience the diversity of life and see the unchanging thread that connects our differences.

If you are not feeling giddy and would still like to know more, please contact Sarah at sarah@thebirdinhand.ca

www.ingramcontent.com/pod-product-compliance
Lightning Source LLC
Chambersburg PA
CBHW051608120626
46551CB00014B/1718